T0091160

MY POCKET
GRATITUDE

MY POCKET
GRATITUDE

ANYTIME EXERCISES FOR AWARENESS,
APPRECIATION, AND *JOY*

COURTNEY E. ACKERMAN
AUTHOR OF *MY POCKET POSITIVITY*

ADAMS MEDIA
NEW YORK LONDON TORONTO SYDNEY NEW DELHI

Adams Media
An Imprint of Simon & Schuster, Inc.
57 Littlefield Street
Avon, Massachusetts 02322

First Adams Media trade paperback edition November 2019

ADAMS MEDIA and colophon are trademarks of Simon & Schuster.

For information about special discounts for bulk purchases, please contact Simon & Schuster Special Sales at 1-866-506-1949 or business@simonandschuster.com.

The Simon & Schuster Speakers Bureau can bring authors to your live event. For more information or to book an event contact the Simon & Schuster Speakers Bureau at 1-866-248-3049 or visit our website at www.simonspeakers.com.

Manufactured in China

10 9 8 7 6 5 4 3 2 1

Library of Congress Cataloging-in-Publication Data
Names: Ackerman, Courtney E., author.
Title: My pocket gratitude / Courtney E. Ackerman, author of My Pocket Positivity.
Description: Avon, Massachusetts: Adams Media, 2019.
Series: My pocket.
Identifiers: LCCN 2019015816 | ISBN 9781507211014 (pb) | ISBN 9781507211021 (ebook)
Subjects: LCSH: Self-actualization (Psychology) | Motivation (Psychology) | Happiness. | BISAC: SELF-HELP / Personal Growth / Happiness. | SELF-HELP / Motivational & Inspirational.
Classification: LCC BF637.S4 A3445 2019 | DDC 179/.9--dc23
LC record available at https://lccn.loc.gov/2019015816

ISBN 978-1-5072-1101-4
ISBN 978-1-5072-1102-1 (ebook)

CONTENTS

CHAPTER 2:
EXERCISES TO CULTIVATE GRATITUDE
TOWARD YOUR BODY / 39

CHAPTER 3:
EXERCISES TO CULTIVATE GRATITUDE FOR OTHERS / 65

CHAPTER 4:
EXERCISES TO CULTIVATE GRATITUDE
FOR YOUR PAST AND PRESENT / 91

CHAPTER 5:
EXERCISES TO CULTIVATE GRATITUDE
FOR YOUR SURROUNDINGS / 117

CHAPTER 6:
EXERCISES TO CULTIVATE GRATITUDE
IN DIFFICULT TIMES / 143

INTRODUCTION

* Do you want to learn how to maximize your happiness?
* Are you looking for ways to be appreciative of what you have?
* Do you want to improve your mental health and your self-esteem, and bring more good things into your life?

If you answered yes to any of these questions, you picked the right book!

My Pocket Gratitude gives you 150 exercises you can do at home, at work, or on the go to help you see all the good around you, notice the little things, stay open to the positive, and adopt a more grateful perspective. It is an excellent resource whether you have never practiced gratitude exercises as a regular part of your day or if you are an experienced practitioner who needs a few new ideas.

This helpful guide will provide you with quick but powerful exercises that you can incorporate into your daily life to cultivate a greater sense of gratitude for:

* Yourself
* Your body
* Others

* Your past and your present
* Your surroundings
* Some of the most difficult situations in life

As you delve into these exercises, keep in mind that they don't follow a strict order. If you feel drawn to one topic in particular, skip straight to it. The rest will be here waiting for you whenever you are ready.

If you put in just a little bit of time and effort, you'll find that practicing gratitude will not only make you more grateful; it will also make you happier and even healthier. Flip to any page in this book if you need a dose of gratitude, and you'll find a quick and simple way to get it!

CHAPTER 1

EXERCISES TO CULTIVATE SELF-GRATITUDE

In this chapter, you will learn twenty-five different ways to enhance your gratitude for yourself. Increasing your self-gratitude is one of the most important goals you can set and is one of the most impactful ways to channel your time and energy. These exercises will walk you through several ways to target your gratitude for yourself, including focusing on your strengths, practicing gratitude-focused mindfulness, treating yourself with love and understanding, and reminding yourself of the good things you have done. Spend just a few minutes a day practicing these exercises, and you will see what a difference they can make to your self-love and self-gratitude.

SAY "THANK YOU"
TO YOURSELF

It's funny that the person we so often forget to thank is the person we should be showing constant gratitude to: ourselves! It's important to remember to show yourself some gratitude, as that self-gratitude is what forms the foundation for the more all-encompassing gratitude that can be such a life-changing force.

If the idea of saying "thank you" to yourself sounds strange, try this: Imagine there is someone who caters to your every need. He or she pays your bills, picks up your groceries, runs your errands, makes your meals, washes your dishes, does your laundry, and cleans your home. Would you say "thank you" to this person for taking care of these tasks and chores for you? If it seems obvious to say "thank you" to someone else, then it should also be obvious to thank *yourself* for taking care of the same things!

Follow these steps to give yourself some sincere thanks:

1. Think of all the things you do that are necessary parts of life but that you don't particularly enjoy (e.g., the mundane activities listed previously).
2. Consider the time and effort that goes into completing these tasks.
3. Say "thank you" to yourself and extend your sincere gratitude to yourself for doing all of these unpleasant things.

FOCUS ON APPRECIATING YOUR STRENGTHS

One of the best ways to feel more self-gratitude is to focus on some of the best things about yourself—in other words, your strengths. After all, it's hard to appreciate something if you're constantly thinking about what's *wrong* with it!

The same goes for appreciating yourself: The more you focus on the good things about yourself, the easier it will be to feel grateful for who you are instead of feeling down about who you're *not*.

To focus on your strengths, try these steps:

1. When you start comparing yourself to others, feeling low about a mistake you made, or feeling down about not measuring up to some arbitrary standard, pause.
2. Ask yourself, "What is one of my strengths?" or "What is one of the best things about myself?" Take a minute to think about a strength or your favorite aspect of yourself, like being highly organized or good at relating to others.
3. Try showing yourself some gratitude for your strength; say something like, "I am grateful to myself for being [your strength]" or "I am grateful that I can [your strength]."

Remind yourself to come up with one strength every time your brain wants to highlight a weakness. After a while, you'll have trained yourself to think about your strengths first and your weaknesses second—if you think about them at all!

This focus on your strengths will prime you for greater self-appreciation and make it easier to feel self-gratitude.

EXPRESS YOUR GRATITUDE TO A HIGHER POWER

If you want a quick boost of gratitude and you believe in any sort of higher power—God, another benevolent deity, any sort of all-present and unseen entity, or the universe itself—this is a great exercise to practice.

To give it a try, follow these steps:

1. Take a few minutes by yourself in a quiet space. Limit the interruptions: Silence your phone, turn off the TV, and get someone else to watch the kids for a bit.
2. Think about your life and all that is good in it. Think about your relationships, your career, your family, your hobbies, your strengths and talents, your achievements and the things you are most proud of yourself for, and anything else that makes your life enjoyable and meaningful.
3. Wrap up all this goodness into a little package of gratitude for everything you are and everything you have, and send it up to whatever higher power you believe in.
4. Thank the higher power for the gifts you have been given. Try something like this, "Thank you for everything you have given me. I recognize that my life is full of love, joy, and wonderful experiences, and I am grateful for each and every one of them."
5. Now extend this gratitude to yourself. Thank yourself for taking the time to practice gratitude and give yourself a metaphorical pat on the back (or a real one—your choice!) for doing something good for *you*.

"CATCH" SOMEONE ELSE'S GRATITUDE TOWARD YOU

Have you ever noticed that most contagious things are considered to be bad? When you think of the word *contagious*, you probably think of things like a cold, a flu, a rash, or even one of the more serious bacteria-fueled ailments.

But do you know what else can be contagious? Gratitude!

It's true, you can "catch" gratitude if you set your mind to it. In this exercise, you'll learn how to pick up on someone else's gratitude toward you and embrace it. Here's how:

1. Wait and watch for someone to show you gratitude. Here's a handy tip: To speed this step up, go out of your way to do something kind for another person!
2. When you notice that you're on the receiving end of someone's gratitude—no matter how seemingly small or insignificant—stop and recognize it!
3. Feel their gratitude, "catch" it as it comes your way, and savor it. Allow yourself to feel good about helping someone else, and enjoy the sensation of vicarious gratitude.
4. To let gratitude really take hold, remind yourself that you deserve it. Tell yourself you're a good person who does good things, and that you are completely justified in accepting and embracing that gratitude.

Sometimes all you need to boost your self-gratitude is to give yourself permission to like and appreciate who you are—and having someone else lead the charge makes this even easier!

CREATE
A GRATITUDE PLAN

It might sound strange, but there's nothing odd about planning out your gratitude! Sometimes making a plan to be grateful can be exactly what you need; it keeps you on track and accountable, and it takes away some of the pressure to come up with an exercise or practice on the spot.

A journal or notebook that you write in regularly makes a great place for your plan, or you can type it up on your laptop or enter it into an app on your phone.

Here are some guidelines to follow in developing your gratitude plan:

* **Be specific.** Write down what you will do, how long you will do it, and when you will do it. Being too vague is a good way to set yourself up for forgetting or skipping a practice.
* **Be consistent.** Don't plan just one gratitude activity a week. Try to work in at least one a day.
* **Mix it up.** Don't do the same exercise or practice every day, all week. Throw in a new one and try exercises that you wouldn't normally do.
* **Stick to it!** This is the hardest step of all, but it's also the most important. Try noting it on your calendar or setting an alarm to help you remember.

You can use the exercises in this book and organize them in your plan however you like, or you can find other exercises and practices online.

WRITE A LIST OF YOUR POSITIVE TRAITS

Did you know that you're pretty loveable? It's true; there's a lot to love about you!

If you already believe it, great! You can make it official by writing it down. If you don't believe it, no problem! This exercise will help you realize that you have a lot to be grateful to yourself for.

Grab a pen and some paper and get ready. This list is going to help you realize why you're awesome, and why you should be thanking yourself for being awesome.

1. At the top, write "Why I'm Awesome" or "Why I'm Loveable" or any other title that captures how you want to feel about yourself.
2. Now, get to listing! Think about all the awesome things about yourself. Don't worry if you can't think of big things right away; just start with the small stuff.
   * For example, are you a kind and thoughtful person? Write it down!
   * Do you have a knack for making people laugh? Write "hilarious" down!
   * Have you ever given someone an amazing gift they absolutely loved? You'd better be writing "I'm a fantastic gift-giver" on the list!
3. Go on listing reasons why you're awesome until you run out of reasons, you run out of space to write them, or your hand starts to cramp up.

Now, read the list to yourself and think about what a great person it describes. Thank yourself for being so great, and mean it!

THANK YOURSELF FOR THINKING AHEAD

Remember that time you planned ahead and things went just swimmingly? Maybe it happened only a day or two ago and you're still basking in the afterglow of your good decision-making, or maybe you're thinking back a few weeks or months to such a time.

Whenever it happened, hold on to that experience and harness it to boost your gratitude toward yourself. Here's how:

1. Think about the situation and remember all the details—what was happening, why you needed to plan ahead, what you needed to plan for, and so on.
2. Detail the steps you took to prepare yourself. How did you decide what you needed to do? What concrete actions did you take?
3. Think about how everything panned out. What were the benefits of planning ahead? What outcomes would not have materialized—or would have been significantly less positive—if you hadn't planned ahead?
4. Give yourself your sincerest thanks for planning ahead. Say something like, "Thank you, self, for thinking ahead and setting me up to succeed. You're the best!"

When you take the time to remember the good things you have done, whether for yourself or others, you find it much easier to foster self-love and self-gratitude. Remind yourself that you did something good for you and how good that felt, and commit to doing it again to cultivate even greater self-gratitude.

PRACTICE GRATITUDE-FOCUSED MINDFULNESS

Mindfulness is an excellent practice—it helps you to get centered, to root yourself in the present, and to appreciate what you have.

However, you can tweak your mindfulness practice a bit to maximize your gratitude. Take these steps to practice gratitude-focused mindfulness:

1. Find somewhere quiet and peaceful to simply sit with your thoughts for a bit.
2. Close your eyes and focus on your breath for a few moments. Don't try to control it or change it, just observe it as it flows into and out of your lungs. Be grateful for your lungs and your breath.
3. Expand your awareness to your inner thoughts. Listen to them as they drift by, but let them keep on drifting right out of your mind. Observe as new thoughts come in, and refrain from judgment or "should"-ing.
4. Cultivate gratitude for your awareness, for your thoughts, and for the simple ability to think.
5. Expand your awareness once more to use your ears, your nose, and your sense of touch. Notice all the sounds, smells, and sensations you are experiencing. Decide to be grateful for every single thing, and for your ability to experience every single thing.
6. Open your eyes slowly, keeping your present-moment awareness. Look around you, and make the decision to be grateful for everything you see.

ACKNOWLEDGE YOUR OWN EFFORT

How often do you take a moment to think about how much effort you put into each day? I don't mean the effort you put into just one thing, like a project at work or a task at home, but *all* of your many efforts. If you're like most people, you expend quite a bit of effort just to survive and keep yourself sane, clothed, fed, and nurtured.

The fact that you are reading this sentence right now shows that, on top of all this daily effort required to simply continue being a human being, you are willing to put even *more* effort into becoming a better human being.

Use this exercise as an opportunity—or an excuse, if you feel you need one—to acknowledge your own effort and enhance your appreciation for yourself.

Here's how:

1. Take a minute to think about all the effort you put in on a daily basis just to *be*.
2. Now think about the extra effort you're putting in to practice gratitude. It might not seem like much, but remember that it stacks on top of all the work you already do.
3. Remind yourself that not everyone puts in this much effort—or any effort at all—to better themselves, but you are!
4. Thank yourself for doing the legwork and making time to practice more gratitude, an effort that will lead to a healthier, happier you and will reverberate out into your life.

SCHEDULE
A DATE WITH YOURSELF

One of the best ways to show others that you love and appreciate them is to share one of your most precious resources with them: your time. Money can be earned, things can be bought and sold, but your time cannot ever be recovered; if you make a conscious decision to spend time with someone, you're telling them in unequivocal terms that they are valuable and dear to you.

Extend this same appreciation to yourself by spending time with you! Plan to take yourself on a date that you will love. After all, you're the perfect person to plan a date for yourself—you already know everything you enjoy doing, where you enjoy going, and what you enjoy eating and drinking!

Follow these guidelines to take yourself on a date:

* **Set it in stone.** This means scheduling it in your calendar, marking yourself "busy" during that time, and even creating reminders so you don't forget.
* **Plan it out.** Not every moment needs to be filled with activities, but make sure you have something actually planned (e.g., don't just write "hang out with self" on your calendar).
* **Make it enjoyable.** Is doing laundry, cleaning the house, or stopping for coffee while you run errands a good date? No! Plan activities that are actually enjoyable.
* **Don't flake.** It doesn't feel good to be stood up, so don't do it to yourself! Keep your date, no matter what.

CATCH YOURSELF CRITICIZING AND REPLACE IT WITH GRATITUDE

Are you good at observation? Do you catch things other people miss? If so, put your skills to use with this exercise. If not, use this exercise to build those valuable skills.

Your objective is to catch something that can be really sneaky and difficult to detect: your inner critic. We all have one (and we all hate it), and it's normal to find it criticizing us every now and then; however, if your inner critic is getting too loud and overbearing, it's time to catch it in the act and confront it.

Keep an ear out for any self-criticism that pops up in your head. This is the toughest part, since it can easily blend in with the rest of your thoughts. Look for words like *should* or *ought* in your inner monologue to catch it. For example, you might think something like, "I can't believe I said something so stupid to my friend! I should keep my mouth shut."

When you catch it, give your inner critic a scolding. Tell it to lay off, then replace the criticism with self-gratitude. For example, in response to the previous criticism you might say, "I said something I wish I hadn't, but I'm glad I can forgive myself for it, and I'm grateful for my ability to notice it and apologize for it."

This exercise takes some practice, so don't worry if you aren't great at it right away—just keep trying!

CHECK YOUR SELF-CRITICISM AT THE DOOR

Being able to criticize yourself is not necessarily a bad thing; it's healthy to be able to get some perspective and see yourself clearly, warts and all.

Self-criticism becomes harmful when it happens too frequently, and when it doesn't take your strengths and your wins into consideration.

To ensure you are keeping a balanced perspective on yourself and allowing self-gratitude to flourish, try checking your self-criticism at the door.

Here's how to do it:

1. Designate a room in your home where you're not allowed to criticize yourself, even if it's only for a day. Pick a room you spend at least an hour or two in every day.
2. Imagine a "criticism check" at the door of this room, like a coat check at a nice restaurant or club. Instead of checking your coat, you'll check your criticism.
3. Walk through the door to the no-criticism room and visualize taking off your self-criticism and leaving it behind.
4. While in this room, do not criticize yourself for any reason. Remember that it will always be there waiting for you if you need to do some critical reflection, but you don't need to do it right now.

Allow yourself to enjoy the no-criticism room as often as you like during your day, and thank yourself for the chance to simply be, without the distractions of self-criticism.

LIST THE WAYS YOU HAVE POSITIVELY IMPACTED OTHERS

If you're feeling a little down about yourself or having trouble finding extra gratitude for yourself, one excellent way to boost your self-appreciation is by thinking of all the ways you have positively impacted the lives of others. It's often easier to be grateful to yourself when you take a more objective, external perspective on your positive deeds.

Get a notepad or your journal and something to write with, then follow these steps to turn your good deeds into self-gratitude:

1. Think about the nicest thing you have ever done for someone, and write down a short description of it.
2. Think of a time you took action to improve someone's life, and write that down too.
3. List a time when you celebrated something important with a friend or family member (e.g., wedding, graduation) and received their sincere thanks for joining in the celebration.
4. Now that you have the hang of it, continue listing ways that you have positively impacted the lives of others.
5. When you're finished, take a few moments to read over your list and dwell on each good deed you have engaged in. Think about how it impacted the other person(s), and thank yourself for taking positive action.

ALLOW YOURSELF AN EXTRA HELPING

Dieting may be the least effective way to show yourself gratitude.

Of course, feeding your body healthy food and keeping your overall calorie intake in check is not a bad thing; however, the usual ethos of dieting seems to be depriving, chastising, and even punishing yourself. That's no way to develop and maintain a healthy sense of gratitude!

Instead, try taking a different approach to food that might help with getting healthy *and* enhancing your sense of gratitude toward yourself.

When you want an extra helping, a snack, or an indulgent treat, allow yourself to have it.

It's a pretty simple technique, but there is a catch: Only allow yourself to have it if it's what you really, *truly* want.

To find out if it's what you really, *truly* want, pause for a moment.

Ask yourself these three questions:

1. Am I still hungry?
2. Do I just want it because it's there?
3. Is it *really* good enough to warrant a second helping?

If your answers to these three questions indicate that it's worth it, go for it! If not, at least you'll know that you thought it through and made a good decision.

You'll thank yourself for it.

WRITE A
SELF-GRATITUDE LETTER

You may have heard about the gratitude letter exercise. It's pretty popular, and with good reason. It involves writing a heartfelt letter of gratitude to someone in your life and reading it to them or sending it to them. Writing a gratitude letter is a great way to increase your gratitude for others (more on that in Chapter 3), but there's another gratitude letter you should consider writing: a self-gratitude letter.

You can write a self-gratitude letter in much the same way you would write a letter of gratitude to another person, just with a different recipient.

To write your self-gratitude letter, follow these steps:

1. Get some paper and a pen to write with, and address the letter "Dear [your name]."
2. Start your letter with "Thank you for being you."
3. Now take a few moments to think about what you're grateful to yourself for. Are you feeling thankful for your extra-intensive efforts at work lately? Do you want to pat yourself on the back for getting to the gym four times a week over the last month?
4. Expand on your "thank you" by mentioning each of the things you're grateful to yourself for in your letter.
5. Finish the letter with another reminder of your overall gratitude to yourself, and sign it with sincerity.

Go back and read this letter whenever you need a quick boost of self-gratitude.

DROP YOUR "SHOULD" STATEMENTS

The word *should* is a tricky one. It can be helpful, like when you say, "I should be there by six" or "You should check your tire pressure, it looks low."

It can also be extremely unhelpful, like when you tell yourself, "I should not feel this way" or "I should be stronger."

This second usage of *should* doesn't do you any favors. Don't feel bad if you say these things—we all do sometimes! But if you want to develop more gratitude for yourself, you need to learn how to drop your "should" statements. This exercise can help.

To get started, think of a "should" that you catch yourself thinking a lot. Let's use the previous example, "I should not feel this way."

Ask yourself these three questions:

1. Does telling myself, "I should not feel this way" change the reality?
2. Does telling myself, "I should not feel this way" make me feel better?
3. Does telling myself, "I should not feel this way" *positively* motivate me (rather than shame me into taking action)?

I'm guessing you'll probably answer no to each of these questions. If you do, ask yourself why you are still "shoulding" yourself about your feelings when you can clearly see there is no benefit to doing so.

Give yourself a break and allow yourself to feel what you feel, and you will thank yourself for it.

CREATE A SELF-GRATITUDE STATEMENT

To make sure you have a quick and easy way to inject some self-gratitude into your day at the drop of a hat, try creating a self-gratitude statement.

A self-gratitude statement is something you can use to remind yourself to be grateful, to remind yourself what you have to be grateful for, and to help you get in the right frame of mind to be grateful.

Here's how to create and use a self-gratitude statement:

1. Think of some of your best traits and qualities. There are other exercises in this section that can help you do that.
2. Think of your favorite people in your life, those whom you love and who love you. Consider how they see you and what they are grateful for in you.
3. Take these thoughts and transform them into a gratitude statement. It could be something like, "I am grateful for myself because I am kind and caring to people" or "I am grateful for who I am because I am smart and capable."
4. When you notice you are getting upset with yourself or overwhelmed, bring your focus to your self-gratitude statement. Repeat it and remind yourself to really believe it.

Feel free to create a new self-gratitude statement whenever you'd like to focus on another positive aspect of yourself.

LEAVE YOURSELF
A NOTE

If you ever leave yourself sticky notes as a reminder to get some eggs at the store, make a dentist appointment, or pick up the dry cleaning on the way home, you'll understand the logic behind this exercise.

Even if you have the very best of intentions to practice gratitude, to be more grateful, and to appreciate yourself more, things can slip your mind on occasion. When this happens, be sure to give yourself a break! You're only human, and no matter how hard you try, you will never be perfect.

However, you can take steps to make these slips less frequent. One way is to leave yourself a gratitude note. Your gratitude note is a reminder of not only your intention to practice gratitude but also exactly what you have to be grateful for.

Here's how to write a good gratitude note:

1. Consider what aspect of yourself you would like to cultivate gratitude for (e.g., your hard work, your hope and positivity).
2. Come up with a statement of gratitude focused on this aspect (e.g., "I am grateful for all the hard work I put in to make a better life for myself and my family.").
3. Leave the note somewhere you will see it frequently.

Seeing this note on a regular basis will help you establish self-gratitude as a daily habit.

BEFRIEND
YOURSELF

If you have trouble extending gratitude to yourself—but you have no trouble feeling grateful for your family and friends—this exercise can help you out!

Give it a try by following these steps:

1. Think of a friend who is near and dear to you. Put yourself in their shoes, and try to see out of their eyes.
2. Take a look at yourself from their perspective. Think about what they like about you and what they appreciate about being friends with you. If it helps, put these things down on paper to give yourself more ownership over them.
3. Think about what kind of person this list describes. It probably describes a pretty great person, someone anyone would want to be friends with!
4. Decide to be friends with the person this list describes. If you look at it objectively, it shouldn't be too hard to make that decision.
5. Let that decision to be friends with the person the list describes act as a reminder that you have a lot to offer. Allow yourself to think of that person as a good friend.
6. Acknowledge that that person is you!

It takes a few steps to get to it, but the end result is that you will feel friendlier, more compassionate, and more grateful toward yourself.

BUY YOURSELF
A PRESENT

This is a fun exercise, because you get two good things out of it: a present and more gratitude toward yourself!

It's a fact of life, and has been since the beginning of time, that presents are an excellent way to butter someone up. Take advantage of this fact to butter *yourself* up!

Think of something you've been really wanting—not something you need, just something you want. It should be something fun and totally unnecessary.

Once you have decided what you want, go to the store and buy it! You really should try to go to the store to buy it, as it feels more personal and meaningful that way; however, if it's something you can't get at the store, place your order online.

If you enjoy opening presents, feel free to put in a little extra time or money to get it gift-wrapped. It's even more fun and special to open a present when you have to tear through some wrapping paper or untie some ribbon to get to it!

When you do open it, be sure to give yourself your sincere thanks for the gift.

This exercise will boost gratitude in two ways: It will help you show yourself the self-gratitude you already have, and it will make you feel even more grateful to yourself!

NAMASTE YOUR WAY TO SELF-GRATITUDE

If you practice yoga, you have probably heard the word *namaste*, but you may not know where it comes from and what it actually means.

It's a greeting that comes from Sanskrit and carries with it an element of deep respect and connection at a spiritual level. According to some, it means, "The divine in me bows to the divine in you." Others translate it as a more simple "Salutations to you."

However it's translated, the term has gained new meaning in Western cultures as a message of respect and gratitude. It is usually uttered at the end of a yoga class, acting as a "thank you" to the instructor for their time and effort, and a "thank you" back to the students for sharing their time and space to practice yoga.

Although *namaste* is generally used to show gratitude to others, here's how you can use it to enhance your self-gratitude. When you have done something good for yourself, like prepared a healthy meal, put in some time at the gym, or enforced a healthy boundary, give yourself a *namaste*: Place your hands at your heart center, palms pressed together, and bow. Direct this energy from respect, gratitude, and thankfulness at yourself.

CHANGE UP
YOUR SELF-TALK

How do you talk to yourself? Do you speak with love and kindness? Or do you find yourself constantly belittling, insulting, or criticizing yourself?

It's no small feat to turn your self-talk around, but it is one of the most worthwhile goals to strive toward. It will also be a powerful step toward cultivating a greater sense of gratitude in your life, as you will make your whole outlook on life more positive.

Here's how to do it:

1. Watch for any negative self-talk that crops up. It's a common occurrence during rough times; as you get down about one area in your life, it's easy to become more negative about the rest of it too.
2. For each bit of negative self-talk, ask yourself, "Does this serve me? Does this contribute to a better life for me? Do I benefit from this in any way?" You will likely find that you answer no to each of those questions.
3. Ask yourself, "What kind of self-talk would be more beneficial to me?" Think of ways you can modify or alter the negative self-talk into something positive and beneficial to you, and give it a shot!

Keep practicing, and you'll soon find that feeling gratitude for yourself is a lot easier than it was at first.

CELEBRATE THE BEST PARTS OF YOURSELF

Focusing on the best parts of yourself is an effective way to enhance your self-gratitude. It's easier to be grateful when you have a long list of things to be grateful for!

If you haven't already done so, now might be a good time to flip back a few pages and complete the "Focus On Appreciating Your Strengths" and the "Write a List of Your Positive Traits" exercises; these will give you a good base list to help you think about the best parts of yourself.

If you haven't completed these exercises and you want to get right to it, spend a few minutes thinking about what is best in you—your most honorable traits and favorite personality features. Make a list of at least five to ten things.

Once you have your list, whether by completing the two exercises mentioned or by putting it together on the fly, go through it one by one and celebrate it! Give yourself a pat on the back for each item on your list, and try to be truly sincere in telling yourself that each trait and feature is an accomplishment and something to be proud of.

When you tell yourself such nice things and celebrate yourself, it's easy to feel a little more self-gratitude.

PLAN
A SOLO TRIP

Have you ever traveled by yourself? If you have, you'll understand why this is such a great way to boost your self-gratitude.

When you only have yourself to count on, it's amazing what you will find yourself capable of doing. Plus, traveling by yourself means you're not on anyone else's schedule; you can decide what you want to do and when you want to do it!

You don't even need to actually go on a trip by yourself—although you definitely should at some point—but taking some time to plan out a perfect solo trip might help you discover an interesting new side of yourself.

Think about these things while planning your trip:

* **Your ideal spot.** Have you always wanted to visit Scotland? Or maybe you're dying to see New Zealand? Think of a place you would love to visit.
* **Your time frame.** When do you want to go? Is the country you're thinking about visiting particularly beautiful during certain seasons? How soon can you make it?
* **Your excursions.** Think about what you would like to do while you're there. Of course, you'll want to try the local cuisine, but are there other activities you want to try? List them.

Now that you have planned your perfect solo trip, take a peek at prices and see if you can actually do it! If you can't afford it right now, don't be discouraged—create a budget that will allow you to take your trip at a specified future date.

DO SOMETHING TOTALLY NEW AND UNEXPECTED

This exercise is similar to the previous one ("Plan a Solo Trip") in that they both enhance your gratitude through showing you that you are a strong, capable, and competent person, and that you can be independent and spontaneous.

To get that boost of self-appreciation without planning a whole trip, try doing something new—and not just something new, but something that nobody would expect from you.

For example, if you've never been a very athletic person, consider joining a "just for fun" soccer or softball league. If you're usually quiet and shy, do some karaoke in a full bar. If you're a practical, risk-averse person, try skydiving, bungee jumping, or some other adrenaline-filled activity.

Engaging in an activity that is totally out of your wheelhouse not only gives you an opportunity to try something new and meet new people; it helps you show yourself that you are brave, adventurous, and willing to try new things!

Whatever you decide to do, make sure to thank yourself when you try your new thing. If it helps, follow this script: "[Your name], thank you for being brave and trying something new. It was scary/difficult/awkward, but it was so worth it!"

Chapter 2

EXERCISES TO CULTIVATE GRATITUDE TOWARD YOUR BODY

In this chapter, your focus will turn to cultivating gratitude for your body. Your body forms the physical basis of who you are and allows you to interact with the world around you. You may not always appreciate every part of your body, but you can learn to appreciate what it is capable of and learn to accept even those things you don't like. These exercises will walk you through twenty-five ways to do this, including pampering yourself, getting some physical activity, trying your hand at yoga, feeding your body healthy food, and simply talking kindly to yourself. Read on to learn more!

GO FOR A
PEACEFUL WALK

Often, the best thing you can do for your body is to take it for a gentle walk and listen to what it has to say, so to speak.

We spend a lot of time *not* listening to our bodies, and that doesn't do us any favors.

To develop greater understanding of, and gratitude for, your body and all that it does for you, try going on a peaceful walk. A peaceful walk is different from a normal walk. On a peaceful walk, your aim isn't to burn calories or improve your cardiovascular health (although those are welcome bonuses of all physical activity), nor is your goal to get from A to B as quickly as possible. Your goal is to embrace your body and enjoy spending time with it.

It might sound odd to talk about spending time with your body—as if you could spend time away from it! But how often do you take some time to simply enjoy being in your own skin, or to appreciate your body and what it can do for you? If you're like most people, probably not very often—if at all.

To try a peaceful walk, map out a short route (about a ten- to twenty-minute walk), wear some comfortable clothing, and get to stepping. Feel each footstep and each swing of your arms. Be present in your body, and cultivate gratitude for your body's amazing abilities with each step you take.

PRACTICE
GENTLE YOGA

Yoga is not only an excellent way to improve your physical health and well-being; it's also a great way to develop more gratitude for your body.

The core ideas in yoga are to get more connected to your body and to the ground you walk on, to find your center, to calm the mind and energize the spirit, and to develop a healthier mental state. One of the ways yoga brings about such great outcomes is by encouraging gratitude for yourself and your body.

If you've ever tried yoga, you know that the movements are generally slow and measured, and that you are encouraged to engage in each movement with mindfulness and awareness of your body and its needs. What better way to show gratitude to your body than to be attentive to its needs?

If you don't have the time or funds to try a yoga class right now, try moving slowly between moves like:

* Balasana (Child's Pose)
* Savasana (Corpse Pose)
* Sukhasana (Easy Pose) or Siddhasana (Accomplished Pose)
* Uttanasana (Standing Forward Fold)
* Paschimottanasana (Seated Forward Bend)
* Baddha Konasana (Bound Angle Pose)

Look up these poses online or ask a friend knowledgeable in yoga to help you out. As you move through the poses, keep your focus on steady breathing and on how your body feels.

In each pose, take a moment to thank your body for the amazing things it can do—including these poses!

SET A
GRATITUDE INTENTION

If you're a fan of yoga, you probably already know all about intentions. If not, just think of an intention as part goal, part promise, and part encouragement. People often set an intention at the beginning of a yoga class to help them keep their goals in mind and stay motivated throughout the class.

If you practice yoga, try using a gratitude intention for a practice.

If you're not interested in practicing yoga, you can still try out a gratitude intention. When you are about to engage in an activity that will make you happier, healthier, or more well-rounded (think working out, self-care, or challenging yourself to boost your skills), follow these simple steps:

1. First, think of your intention and come up with the words you will say to yourself. You might say, "My intention is to show myself gratitude for [whatever activity you are about to engage in]" or "I intend to be more grateful for what my body can do."
2. Once you have an intention in mind, say it to yourself—in your head or out loud—and commit to following through with it.
3. As you go about your activity of choice, if you find your mind wandering or bucking against your intention, gently guide it back to alignment with your intention. For example, if you catch yourself thinking, "I'm so out of shape," push this thought away and replace it with, "I'm grateful to myself for putting in this effort."

TRY MINDFUL JOGGING
(OR RUNNING, OR SKIPPING)

To be more grateful for your body, try some mindful jogging; although, as the title suggests, you don't necessarily need to jog—you can run, walk, jump-rope, skip, army-crawl, and so on. The important aspect of this exercise is that you are doing something physical and active and that you are mindful as you do it.

Here's how to go about it:

1. Lace up your sneakers and get ready to go jogging as you normally would—but ditch the earbuds this time. Plan your route or follow a well-worn path so you don't have to think about it too much.
2. Start out with a moderate pace. As you take each step, pay attention to how it feels to your body.
3. For the first few steps, think about how your feet and ankles feel. Focus on your foot meeting the ground and the movement in your ankle as you angle your foot for another step.
4. For the next few steps, think about how your shins and calves feel—the slight tensing as you take each step.
5. Next, think about your knees, then your thighs, then your hips, buttocks, abdomen, and so on, all the way up to your head.
6. Think about the coordination and communication between brain and body that is needed for you to jog. Think about how much of this is automatic, and how much you take for granted.
7. Offer your body gratitude for its truly amazing ability to jog.

GET YOUR
BODY A GIFT

What's a great way to show someone your love and affection for them, or to show them you're grateful? Getting them a gift!

Both giving and receiving gifts can bring you such good feelings. Take advantage of that fact and cultivate some good feelings *and* gratitude by getting a gift for your body.

This gift should obviously be something you like, but make sure it follows these two important guidelines:

1. It *feels* good to your body.
2. It *does* good for your body.

This means that greasy, calorie-bomb fast food wouldn't qualify as an appropriate gift, since it doesn't do good for your body. It also means that a body-waxing package wouldn't qualify either—because that certainly doesn't feel good!

The right gift for your body will depend on your needs and preferences, but here are a few good suggestions:

* A relaxing or invigorating massage
* A new set of comfortable workout clothes
* A well-fitting pair of running shoes
* A moisturizing and great-smelling lotion

There are lots of terms for an exercise like this: Treat yourself, splurge on yourself, do something good for *you*, and so on. They all amount to the same thing—getting your body a gift. Just be sure the gift is something that feels good *and* does good for your body!

MAKE PEACE
WITH THE MIRROR

Making peace with the mirror can be easier said than done. And the truth is that it doesn't happen overnight. It takes time and effort, but it is possible!

Here's how:

1. First, stand in front of the mirror. Make sure there's some good lighting—this won't work if you can't see yourself!
2. Look at your reflection. Look at your body in particular, from your feet up to the top of your head.
3. Ask yourself what you see when you look at your body. You might see your best features, your "problem areas," strengths, flaws, and parts of your body that you think are just okay.
4. Acknowledge all of that, then say out loud: "It's okay not to be perfect." Repeat it a few times to make sure it really sinks in.
5. Shift your mind-set from what your body looks like to what it allows you to do. When you look at your legs, see yourself walking, running, and jumping. Look at your arms and think of working, picking up your children, or swimming. Continue this for each part of your body.
6. Thank each part for the things it allows you to do. Imagine not being able to do those important and meaningful things, and suddenly the way that part looks will seem much less important.

Now when you look in the mirror, you'll be practiced in seeing function instead of just form.

CONSIDER WHAT YOUR BODY CAN DO

Have you ever thought about everything your body can do? I mean, really thought about it? If you have, you know what it means when people say that our bodies are absolutely, astoundingly capable.

If you find yourself spending a lot of time thinking about what your body *can't* do or what your body looks like, give this exercise a try. You can practice it anytime, but you might find it most helpful after a workout or other physical activity.

If you just completed a workout, went for a run, or even just chased your kids around the yard, take a few minutes to think about all the work that activity entailed. Note each individual action that needed to happen for you to accomplish what you did.

For example, if you played tag with your children, consider that you needed to be able to stand, walk, run, shift directions, move while looking behind you, modulate your speed as needed to escape (or to allow a young child to catch you), and most likely the ability to talk and laugh while doing all of these things.

As adults, we get so used to what our bodies can do that we stop feeling grateful for all of it. Now that you have a list of all the things your body just did during a particular activity, practice being grateful for each and every ability. Thank your body for empowering you to do something meaningful, like play with your children.

GIVE YOUR BODY
A HEALTHY MEAL

We often gravitate toward unhealthy food when we want to give ourselves a treat. Although the urge is understandable—and totally fine to indulge once in a while—the real treat is to give your body food that is not only delicious but also nutritious and healthy.

To be more thankful for your body and to honor all that it does for you, make it a healthy meal. What's considered healthy will vary by person, but in general try to avoid processed foods, high sugar content, high sodium content, and very high fat content, and include as much fresh produce as you can.

When you're ready to eat your healthy and delicious meal, pause for a quick moment of appreciation. If you like to pray, say a prayer of thanks for the food or simply take a quiet moment to feel grateful for the food and thank the universe, the farmers who grew the food, the people who picked the crops, or anyone or anything else that makes sense to you.

As you eat, focus your mind on how what you are doing will benefit you. Think about how good it is for your body, and how a healthy body contributes to a healthy life and a healthy soul.

Visualize your meal strengthening and sustaining your body. Send your gratitude to your body along with each bite as it travels toward your belly.

WRITE A POSITIVE
HAIKU TO YOUR BODY

Don't worry, you don't need to be a poet to try this exercise! All you need is a willingness to give it a shot.

Haiku originated in Japan and is one of the easiest forms of poetry to write—at least in terms of following the rules. A haiku consists of only three lines: The first and third lines have five syllables, and the second line has seven syllables. Haikus do not use metaphors or similes; instead, they generally convey mood through imagery.

In this exercise, you will create a positive haiku about your body. The guidelines are:

1. It must have three lines: five syllables in the first line, seven syllables in the second line, and five syllables in the third line.
2. It must be about your body.
3. It must be positive.

That's it! Easier said than done, I know. The point is to acknowledge what your body is, and accept and appreciate it for what it is. Think of a way to describe your body and couple that with something it can do. For example, if your body has a little extra weight, try a haiku like this:

"Legs round and shapely
Middle soft and supportive
This body can dance"

It describes a body without judgment and notes something fun you can do with it—a perfectly positive expression of love and gratitude to your body.

INCORPORATE GRATITUDE INTO YOUR STRETCH

If you've ever tried group exercise classes, weight training, running, or just about any physical activity, you've probably been told about the importance of stretching. It's true—stretching is a vital practice for a healthy and happy body, especially when you tend to put it through the wringer in your workouts.

This exercise will give you another reason to stretch, as well as an added benefit: giving your body some gratitude.

When you finish a workout, wake up in the morning, or just feel the need for a stretch, try this:

1. Stretch out your legs however you normally do. Send a wave of gratitude to your legs for their ability to carry you through your day and/or your workout.
2. Stretch your arms as you usually do. Send them some gratitude for allowing you to hold weights, keep time with music as you dance, or prop you up for push-ups.
3. Stretch your back and send it some gratitude for holding everything up and allowing your arms and legs to do what they do.
4. Stretch your neck and shoulders, and thank them for holding up your head. Allow them to release any tension and replace it with gratitude.
5. Finally, do a whole body stretch and revel in the sensation. Be grateful for your body's many wonderful abilities.

Some people like to finish this exercise by hugging themselves, but if that feels awkward for you, do whatever feels right for you and your body.

LIFT
SOME WEIGHTS

If weight lifting isn't your thing, don't sweat it—pun intended! You don't need to become a body builder to reap the benefits of doing a little weight training. Lifting weights will help you realize all that your body is capable of and help you naturally feel more grateful for it.

Here's a beginner's guide to lifting weights for body gratitude:

* Think about your muscles in terms of groups; for example, your calves, quadriceps (front of your thighs), hamstrings (back of your thighs), and buttocks are all in the lower body group. When you work out your lower body, think about trying to include each of the muscles in this group.
* Start small—even smaller than you think! If a weight feels at all heavy, set it aside and save it for later. You should be able to do a dozen repetitions of each move without getting *too* fatigued.
* Make sure to give your whole body some love. Even if there's one area in particular you want to work on, you should still do at least a little bit of work with the rest of your body.
* Be mindful as you exercise. For each repetition, think about what your body is doing and how it's doing it. Keep your mind open to the wonder that is your body!

Most important of all, remember to thank your body for what it can do. Show it gratitude by making it stronger and healthier.

DO A CARTWHEEL
OR SOMERSAULT

As children, we did things like cartwheels all the time. Do you remember playing tag, doing somersaults, leaping as high as you could, and pushing yourself so high on the swings that you almost went above the top of the swing set?

We are so physical and in tune with our bodies when we are young. Unfortunately, we often start to lose this sense of presence in our bodies as we age. Putting yourself back into your childhood shoes (metaphorically, of course) is one of the best ways to get that sense back and enhance your appreciation of your body and what it can do.

If you barely remember what a cartwheel is or have no idea how to do it, not to worry! You don't need to do a perfect cartwheel to reap the benefits of feeling childlike again. Just give it your best shot—bonus points if you're outside on the grass!

If doing a cartwheel isn't your thing or simply isn't feasible for your body at this time, that's okay. Try doing a somersault instead. It's a bit easier than a cartwheel and can make you feel just as childlike and spontaneous.

Let your inner child out to play, and he or she will thank you with a greater appreciation for your body.

GO
DANCING

When is the last time you went out dancing? When is the last time you danced at all?

Many of us have enjoyed going out dancing at some point in our lives, but most of us probably haven't been in years. If you always enjoyed dancing and can't remember the last time you did it, this is the perfect exercise for you. If you were never a huge fan of dancing in front of people, don't worry—you can dance all by yourself!

So go out dancing (or stay in dancing), but remember to keep the focus on gratitude:

* With each dance move you lay down, think about how much it takes for your body to do it. Think about all the tiny little movements that go into it, and how your body moves seamlessly from one to the next.
* Think about how good it feels to let loose once in a while! Even if you're not a fan of the expressive movement sort of dance, you can surely understand how great it feels to put your feelings on display through body movement.
* Thank your body for each and every dip, slide, and shake. Remind yourself of all the wonderful ways in which you can put your body to good use, including dancing.

TRY A NEW
PHYSICAL ACTIVITY

Is there something you've wanted to try for a long time but never got up the courage or found the time to do it? Maybe you really want to try kickboxing, or you're curious about Zumba. Perhaps you've been eyeballing a CrossFit gym in the neighborhood, or you find yourself feeling envious of all those happy, sweaty people coming out of a cycling class.

Whatever it is, ask yourself this: "Why haven't I done it yet?"

If your answer is something like "I'm scared to look silly" or "It will be too hard," then you'll know it's the perfect activity for this gratitude-boosting exercise!

Sign up for the class or get a free trial to the gym, and give it a shot. You don't need to make any long-term commitments yet; just commit to giving this one class your all.

As you cycle, dance, or sprint your way through the activity, keep two thoughts running through your head. If you need to, feel free to metaphorically shove out other thoughts to make room for these two:

1. "My body really can do this!"
2. "I'm so grateful that my body can do this."

Keeping this running monologue in your head will help you stay motivated, proud, and grateful for yourself, your body's abilities, and your courage to try something new.

ACKNOWLEDGE AND CONFRONT YOUR NEGATIVE THOUGHTS

It never feels good to think negative thoughts about your body. No one wants to feel ashamed, guilty, or unhappy about the skin they live in.

However, don't make the mistake of burying these thoughts deep down or locking them away. They'll still be there, but they might become even more embedded in your mind.

Instead, take the counterintuitive action: Hear them, listen to them, and acknowledge them.

To acknowledge does not mean to agree, embrace, or embody—it simply means that you confirm these thoughts are there and they are real.

Grab a journal or notebook and write down the thought that's bothering you. Once you have acknowledged your thought and accepted that you are experiencing it, you can move on to the really impactful part of this exercise: confronting it.

Take the thought that's cropping up and deconstruct it. What is the thought getting at? What part of your body is it focused on? Is it focused on function or on form?

Now confront the thought. If it's about a part of your body that's "too big," "not big enough," or any other description of that part, challenge the thought by focusing on function. For example, if your thought is "My thighs are so fat," then say this to yourself: "My thighs carry me everywhere I need to go."

Practice acknowledging and confronting your negative thoughts about your body, and you will find yourself feeling better about and more grateful for your body.

PRACTICE SELF-CARE
FOR YOUR BODY

Do you practice self-care? If not, this exercise is a great opportunity to start!

If you're not familiar with the concept, self-care is engaging in activities that help you improve, maintain, or enhance your mental health and well-being.

Self-care is an effective way to feel more grateful to yourself for all that you do for you. Focus your self-care efforts on your body, and you will reap the rewards, one of which is greater gratitude for your body.

If you're not sure how to practice self-care for your body, here's a list of ideas for you to try:

* Draw yourself a soothing bubble bath.
* Go to your favorite fitness class and work up a sweat.
* Spend fifteen minutes just stretching your entire body.
* Go to a spa and get a massage or a facial.
* Practice a body-focused mindfulness exercise, like a body scan.
* Sit in a sauna and soak in the heat.
* Do some meal planning and prepare healthy meals for your week in advance.

This list is not exhaustive, so feel free to add any body-focused self-care activities you think would be effective. Treat your body well, and you will cultivate a practice of gratitude for your body that will help you lead a healthier and happier life.

MAKE
AN APPRECIATION LIST

You might find it easier to make a list of things you *don't* appreciate about yourself than things you *do* appreciate. If so, you're not alone! Many people struggle to love their body amid body image issues and social pressure.

If this describes you, making an appreciation list is a great way to address these issues.

Get out your notebook or grab some paper and a pen, then follow these steps to create an appreciation list:

1. At the top, write "Things I Appreciate about My Body."
2. Now come up with your list! Think of at least five things you appreciate about your body. These can be about how you look, your abilities, your talents, or anything else that has to do with your body.
3. Write out the items on your list, starting each with "I appreciate..."

Here are a couple of examples to get you started:

* I appreciate my eyes. They're a pretty color, and I think they're one of my best features.
* I appreciate my strong calves. They take me up and down the rolling hills to work each day.
* I appreciate my fingers. They allow me to engage in my talent of playing the piano.

Once you have your list written out, read through it to get an instant boost of appreciation for your body. Return to the list whenever you're feeling down about yourself and allow it to lift your spirits.

EMBRACE
PLEASANT SENSATIONS

Do you love the feel of sand between your toes? Do you feel luxurious when you lie down on a really soft carpet? Do you have a silk robe or particularly soft T-shirt to wear when you want to feel pampered and comfortable?

If none of these sensations float your boat, I bet there are some others you love to feel. Whether it's feeling something soft, smooth, or silky against your skin; enjoying the shivery sensation you get from a small breeze; or warming your hands in front of a fire, reveling in pleasant sensations is one of the best parts of life.

To parlay this fact into greater gratitude for your body, commit to embracing and enjoying these pleasant sensations—really enjoying them, rather than simply noting them and moving on.

While you enjoy whatever sensation you have chosen, be mindful of the experience. Thank your body for its ability to feel the silky rippling of water, the nerves in your skin that respond to a gentle touch, and the muscles that relax and drop all the stress they hold when massaged.

Practice this exercise regularly to stay thankful for your body and its amazing ability to feel all of these wonderful sensations.

TAKE A BREAK
FROM SOCIAL MEDIA

Social media—the ubiquitous thing that connects us all while keeping us apart! It's hard to avoid even if you want to.

There's nothing wrong with using social media, and it's great to have such an easy way to keep up with family and friends; however, you need to be cautious about how you use it, particularly in terms of your body. Seeing too many airbrushed and painstakingly posed pictures on social media can leave you feeling even less loving toward and grateful for your body.

To make sure you don't fall into this trap, try taking a break from social media. Follow these steps to give it a try:

1. Deactivate all your social media profiles. If that's not possible, uninstall them from your phone and remove them from your bookmarks. You can always reinstall and add them back later.
2. Give it at least a few days, and fill your time with something else you enjoy doing. If it's a physical activity, even better.
3. After you've had some time to be without social media, grab your journal and write an entry on how you feel. Consider your feelings toward your body in particular. Do you think you benefited from avoiding the airbrushed and perfectly filtered photos on *Instagram*? Do you feel any more positive about your body since you weren't seeing transformational before-and-after pictures on *Facebook*?

Give yourself some time away from social media, and you'll likely find it's easier to be grateful for the body you have when you're not comparing it to others.

PRACTICE
SUN SALUTATIONS

Sun salutations are not only a great way to get warmed up physically and mentally; they're also an excellent way to remind yourself of your body's amazing abilities and boost your body gratitude.

Here's how to do them:

1. Stand up straight with your arms by your sides.
2. Take a deep breath and raise your arms over your head, then release your breath as you fold forward at the waist.
3. Breathe in as you lift your chest up to the level of your hips, keeping your spine straight.
4. Exhale as you lower your hands to the ground and step your feet back into a Plank Pose.
5. Take another breath, then exhale as you slowly lower your body toward the ground. See if you can hover just above the ground for a moment.
6. Breathe in and push the ground away, curving your spine back and bringing your head and chest up.
7. Let your breath out as you reverse your bend, coming into Downward Dog (hands and balls of your feet on the floor, hips up in an inverted "V").
8. Take a few deep breaths, bend your knees, and step your feet up to your hands, moving into a Standing Forward Fold.
9. Breathe in, stand up straight, and reach your arms out wide, bringing them up and over your head, then letting them float gently back to your sides.

As you finish the exercise, think back on all the movements you engaged in and remind yourself to be grateful for everything your body can do.

LISTEN TO
BODY-POSITIVE SONGS

To find the inspiration you need to feel grateful to your body, go for a tried-and-true method: listening to songs that are body-positive and uplifting.

You might have some songs in mind already; if so, great! Put a few of them on a playlist and listen to them, one after the other, for at least ten minutes or so. While they're playing, get into the spirit! If you feel like jumping up and dancing to them, do it! If you feel like stretching and appreciating your flexibility, do that. If you want to lift some weights or do a couple of household chores to appreciate your strength, go right ahead! Do whatever you need to feel happy, positive, and grateful for your body.

If you're not sure what songs to put on, no worries. Head on over to your favorite browser and type in "body-positive songs." You'll get a ton of good suggestions for songs you can listen to that are constructive and optimistic about all body types.

They won't all be your body-positive anthem, but you're sure to find at least a few good ones that lift your spirits and encourage a healthy sense of love and appreciation for your body.

ENLIST A
BODY GRATITUDE BUDDY

Have you ever enlisted a buddy to help you with personal goals? Some people ask a friend or colleague to be their accountability buddy with issues like eating the right foods, exercising regularly, or quitting smoking. The idea is that when you are feeling weak or low, you can reach out to your buddy for some support, understanding, and maybe even a little tough love and motivation.

The same idea can be applied to practicing anything, really—and gratitude is no exception!

Here's how to find and use a gratitude buddy:

1. Think of a friend, colleague, family member, or even just an acquaintance who might be interested in practicing gratitude more often.
2. Ask this friend if they'll be your gratitude buddy. Explain to them that it works like this:
    * You will commit to supporting and encouraging each other in your efforts toward a more regular gratitude practice. That might mean texting or emailing each other every morning to check in, or perhaps a quick phone call each afternoon.
    * You will be there for your buddy in times of need. If you have a sudden flood of ungratefulness, reach out to your buddy so they can remind you of what you have to be grateful for in the present, and vice versa.

Having a buddy can make embarking on a new adventure and establishing a new practice seem more fun and less lonely; plus, you'll have a friend to be grateful for each day!

JUST "BE"
IN THE MORNING

You know those days when you wake up and you just want to lie there and relax? You think you'd give anything to be able to just turn off your alarm and go back to sleep, and you might even briefly consider quitting that pesky job in order to do it.

Well, use this exercise as an excuse to do just that! Not to quit your job, but to lie in bed and just "be" for a while.

When you wake up, allow yourself a few minutes to simply lie in your comfortable bed and feel *good* being in your body.

You might feel like:

* Stretching all the way from your fingers to your toes.
* Snuggling up to your significant other or your child who crawled into bed during the night.
* Burrowing deep into your bedding like a mouse making a nest.
* Pulling the pillow over your head and burying your face into the bed.
* "Starfishing" (throwing all four limbs out wide and taking up a lot of space in the bed).

If any of that feels good to you, do it! The important thing is to simply enjoy these few minutes of being in your body with nothing to do, nowhere to go, and time to spare. We don't always take the time to simply enjoy being in our own skin, but you'll find that it can be both relaxing and rejuvenating, giving you a renewed sense of gratitude for the body you live in.

SCHEDULE A RECURRING PLEASANT ACTIVITY FOR YOUR BODY

Don't worry if this exercise sounds vague; it's supposed to! The idea is to give you the space to fill in the blank with whatever is most pleasant and enjoyable for you.

Think about the things that are most important to you: family, work, volunteering, health, and so on. When you take a closer look at these things, you'll notice there's something they all have in common—you make time for them! If you want to know where someone's priorities lie, look at where they spend their time.

If you're serious about incorporating more gratitude into your life, make sure you are carving out the time to appreciate and say thanks to your body.

This might mean scheduling a biweekly massage, a monthly facial, or a weekly exfoliation session.

If you're a health nut or fitness enthusiast, you might attend your favorite exercise class twice a week or indulge in a sauna and spa session after each intense workout. Or you might want to go for a weekly run or meet with a trainer for scheduled stretching sessions.

Choose whatever activity sounds best and most pleasant to show your body your appreciation and cultivate even greater gratitude.

USE TOUCH TO
BUILD GRATITUDE

This is a powerful exercise that can leave you feeling more grateful, happier, and more in sync with your body. Use it to harness the power of your touch to build appreciation for your body.

Try one (or all) of these touches to encourage love, appreciation, and gratitude for your body:

* Put your dominant hand over your heart, then lay your other hand on top of your dominant hand. Press them both into your chest a bit and relish the feeling.
* Wrap your arms around yourself, with your hands reaching toward your back on either side. Give yourself a little squeeze.
* Hold your own hand. Gently grasp one hand with your other hand. Caress one hand with the other thumb if that feels right.
* Rub your upper arms with your hands. It will warm you up and make you feel cared for and appreciated.

All of these touches are intended to be the kind that feel great coming from a loved one. The point of the exercise is to realize that you can create these good feelings on your own, no other party required!

Unlock greater gratitude for your body with a gentle, loving touch from your own hands.

CHAPTER 3

EXERCISES TO CULTIVATE GRATITUDE FOR OTHERS

The exercises in this chapter are focused on both developing and enhancing your gratitude for others, and showing and sharing your gratitude for others. This is because sharing and showing our gratitude is, in itself, an excellent way to boost gratitude! The relationship between your thoughts and your actions goes two ways: Your thoughts direct your actions, and your actions influence your thoughts. Acting like you are grateful for others can actually make you *feel* more grateful for others. Besides showing your gratitude, these exercises will also walk you through gratitude journaling, savoring the little moments in life, and appreciating people for who they are.

THANK THEM
FOR THE COMPLIMENT

How often do you find yourself deflecting when someone says something nice about you? If you're like many people, you might find it hard to accept a compliment, even if you respect that person's opinion and trust them to tell the truth.

Although this may seem like a display of modesty and humility, it's generally not a fun or healthy way to be. When you are open to receiving positivity and good feelings from others, you are more open to all the good in life. Instead of rejecting or deflecting the compliments you receive, try this instead: Accept them and give your sincere thanks.

When someone says, "You did so great in that presentation," don't say, "Thanks, but I really stumbled over that third point. I felt so tongue-tied!" or "Oh, stop it! I barely survived."

Instead, try saying something that meets three guidelines:

1. It shows that you truly accept the compliment.
2. It includes an expression of gratitude.
3. It makes the person complimenting you feel good too.

For example: "Thank you so much! You're so kind to come see my presentation."

At first, this might feel really awkward, but you'll get better at it with practice. As you continue to accept the good things people say about you and show sincere gratitude, you allow more and more gratitude to infuse your life.

EXPRESS "OLD" GRATITUDE TO A LOVED ONE

If you'd like to try practicing gratitude toward others but just haven't had a recent experience that warrants a grand grateful gesture, you can always practice gratitude for something that happened a while ago.

Here's how to share "old" gratitude:

1. Think of the occasion or event that you would like to express your gratitude for. This could be for anything—a wonderful gift a family member gave you in the past, a grandparent's poignant advice at a crucial moment, or even a small compliment a friend gave you when you really needed it.
2. Remember as much detail as you can about that occasion. Think about when it happened, where you were, whom you were with, and exactly what the other person said or did. If it helps, you can write this all down in a notebook or journal.
3. Figure out exactly why this moment meant so much to you and what good feelings or actions it spurred in you. For example, maybe some good advice prompted you to take a job that you now love or encouraged you to go on that first date with your now-spouse.
4. Share it! Express your gratitude to this person for what they did and how well the situation turned out.

It doesn't matter if you have already thanked the person for this specific occasion. All that matters is that you feel truly grateful to them and would like to express it to them.

THINK OF ALL THE WAYS
SOMEONE HELPED YOU

If you want to encourage greater gratitude for a specific person in your life, you can extend the previous exercise even further—instead of thinking about just one event or occasion when this person did something good for you, think about *all* the ways they have helped you!

Grab a notebook or some scratch paper, because this is probably going to be a long list:

1. Decide on whom you would like to feel greater gratitude for, and write their name at the top of the list. Since your focus is on people who helped you, this person is likely to be a parent, grandparent, mentor, or teacher, but don't feel constrained to those roles.
2. Take five to ten minutes to just sit and think about what this person has done for you. Anything that pops into your head—big or small—write it down.
3. If you're highly organized, you might enjoy putting all these good things in chronological order, so you have a time line of all the ways this person has enhanced your life.
4. Once your list or time line is complete (or near enough), sit back and read through it one more time. Take a moment or two to remember each occasion and feel grateful for it.
5. When you've finished reading your list, wrap up all that gratitude into one big ball of appreciation for this person.

Feel free to share your gratitude with this person to make it even more impactful.

CREATE A LIST OF
PEOPLE YOU LOVE

Sometimes all it takes for you to feel extremely grateful is a reminder of all the people who love you, and all the people you love.

To remind yourself, grab your notebook or journal and write "People I Love" at the top of the page.

Here are some steps to help you get started if you're not sure where to begin:

1. You can start by listing the very closest people to you: your immediate family. This may include your spouse or significant other, your children, your parents, your grandparents, your siblings, and your in-laws.

2. Expand your circle to find a few more people: your extended family. This could include aunts and uncles, cousins, second cousins, and great-aunts and great-uncles.

3. Now move on to close friends. Think of the friends you spend the most time with and the friends who make you feel happiest and most cherished.

4. Next, think of any colleagues or coworkers, current or past. You may have developed a close relationship with a peer or formed a great mentoring relationship with a boss or subordinate.

5. Finally, think about any other people in your life who bring you joy, who fill your life with fun and meaning, and whom you count among those you love.

Once you've written your list, read it and give a little prayer or statement of thanks for each of these people in your life.

SAY "THANKS"
TO A STRANGER

This exercise is truly as easy as it sounds—all you need to do is say "Thanks" to a stranger!

It's true that saying "thank you" to a stranger is easy, but it's the buildup to this expression of gratitude that can have a real, lasting impact.

In order to complete this exercise, you'll need to be on the lookout for good things that strangers do for you. In a world that's frequently distrustful of strangers and that tends to be self-centered, this is a novel idea for many people. It requires reframing your thoughts, and this is where the real impact of the exercise comes from.

When you open yourself to receiving—and even expecting—good from those around you, you start to find it. It's a feedback loop: The more good you find, the more gratitude you will experience, and the more good you will expect to see.

So instead of saying "thanks" to one stranger and calling it good, challenge yourself to be open to receiving the good from strangers for an entire day. Keep an eye out for anything good that you receive from a stranger, whether it's a quick courtesy, a mindless act of politeness, or something more personal like a compliment or gift.

Operating on the assumption that strangers will be nice and kindhearted might feel strange at first, but it will become second nature with enough practice.

GET OUT OF YOUR OWN HEAD
BY GETTING INTO THEIRS

One of the things that keeps us from feeling grateful and optimistic is our tendency to get too wrapped up in our own heads. We are so often thinking about ourselves—about what we want, what we need, what we have to do later, and so on.

When you stop and consider what's going on in other people's heads, you open yourself up to far greater understanding, compassion, and gratitude.

To try this exercise, follow these steps:

1. Pick someone you are not feeling very connected to or understanding toward. It could be someone you're not feeling in tune with overall, or it could be someone you're just not "getting" in the moment, like a coworker who is causing you frustration.
2. Take a break from being in your own head to get into theirs. Imagine you are them, and think about what is going on in "your" head.
3. If you're having a disagreement or feeling frustrated with this person, try to view the issue from their perspective. Find at least one view on the issue that makes sense to both perspectives.

It can be easy to assume the worst of others, but it doesn't do them *or* you any favors; when you take a moment to think from their perspective, you often find that they're doing the best they can. Luckily, it's pretty easy to feel grateful for those who are doing their best.

WRITE AND DELIVER A LETTER OF THANKS

This is a tried and true method of enhancing the gratitude you feel for others. It's a good way to simultaneously identify and acknowledge something you are extremely grateful for and to express that gratitude in a way that benefits both you and the recipient.

Here's how to do it:

1. **Decide on your target.** It should be someone who did something truly wonderful for you. Think about that one person who gave you a chance when no one else would, or the person who believed in you when you barely believed in yourself.
2. **Recall what this person did in detail.** Write down as much of it as you can—what they did, what they said, how they said it.
3. **Remember how it made you feel then, and think about how it makes you feel now.** Harness the gratitude that bubbles up for this person and use it in the next step.
4. **Write this person a letter explaining what they did for you, what it meant to you, and what the outcome was.** It doesn't matter if this person knows you currently and sees where you are now; explain it all anyway. Put into words exactly how this person changed your life for the better.
5. **Hand-deliver the letter to this person and either have them read it or read it to them.** Reiterate your gratitude in person.

This exercise can have a very emotional and significant impact on both people, so be prepared for it!

ENGAGE IN A GRATEFUL ACT OF KINDNESS

Random acts of kindness are great for so many reasons. Not only do they feel good to receive; they feel good to give, they feel good to witness, and they remind you to be more grateful for what you receive from the world.

This last point is what makes engaging in a random act of kindness a good way to boost your gratitude—showing kindness to someone else is a surefire way to remind yourself of the kind acts you have received.

To try it out, look around you—right this minute—and find one stranger you can do something nice for. If you're struggling to think of something to do, here are some good examples:

* Pay for the drive-through order of the person behind you in line.
* Tell someone who is looking sad or down that you love their shirt, their shoes, their coat, their umbrella, or anything else you might happen to like.
* If someone looks like they're in a big hurry, let them take the next taxi, hold the elevator for them, or do something else to help them get on their way.

After you've engaged in your grateful act of kindness, spend a minute or two reflecting on how it made you feel and how it probably made the other person feel. Remind yourself of how often acts of kindness happen in the world around you, and encourage your sense of gratitude for all this kindness.

SAVOR
THE LITTLE MOMENTS

When you stop to think about it, life really is all about the small stuff.

You shouldn't sweat the small stuff, but you also shouldn't dismiss it entirely! It's the little things that matter most, in the grand scheme of things.

If you appreciate all the little moments and find joy in the less exciting or impactful parts of your day, you will experience more happiness than if you simply float through your day, unmindful of the positive moments happening all around you.

To cultivate more gratitude for others, focus on savoring the little moments with them. Make an effort to notice the small things, the quirks, and the kind words that often go unnoticed. Seek out these things when you share a quiet moment with your loved one or when they don't realize you're watching.

For example, many parents know exactly how to savor the little moments because they do this all the time with their young children. When it seems like they grow up faster than should be possible, it's important to take mental snapshots and maximize your joy in the experience as it unfolds.

Try paying extra attention to the little moments with your loved ones, and be ready to surrender completely to the experience. When you do, you'll experience a rush of love and appreciation for them.

CULTIVATE GRATITUDE
FOR YOUR CHILDREN

Children are one of life's biggest blessings, and as such they're pretty easy to cultivate gratitude for—although they can make it challenging sometimes. It's one thing to be grateful for your children in an abstract way, by thinking about how much you love them and how meaningful they are in your life; it's another to be actively engaged in gratitude for them, even as they press each and every one of your buttons!

Here's how to work on being more grateful for your children:

* Focus on the positive moments with your children. Every child has tantrums once in a while, but limit your consideration to some of the best moments you've had with your children.
* Think about the positive changes to you and your character since having children (e.g., you're more patient, you don't sweat the small stuff anymore).
* Think of the fun things you've had the opportunity to do because of your children (e.g., go to kids' birthday parties, visit Disneyland).
* Consider how unique, special, and completely lovable each of your children is.

Wrap all of these thoughts up into a big package of gratitude for your children and let it soak into you. Feel every little bit of gratitude for your children, and commit to taking it with you wherever you go (and whatever they do).

APPRECIATE HIS OR HER LITTLE QUIRKS

If you're interested in developing more gratitude for a specific person, this exercise can help you do it.

It's all about appreciating the little quirks and personality nuances. It's great to be grateful for the big things—like someone's kindness, honesty, sense of humor, or general helpfulness—but appreciating the small stuff is your secret weapon for cultivating more gratitude for them.

Think of one person in particular you want to appreciate more. It can be anyone, from your significant other to the new guy at work.

Once you have this person in mind, follow these steps:

1. Spend more time with this person as soon as you are able to, and make sure you're actually paying attention and staying mindful when you do.
2. Be on the lookout for any little quirks you can find. For example, maybe she snorts when she laughs, or maybe he does a little finger-drumming on the table during slow moments in conversation.
3. Observe these little quirks and think about how they make us all unique and individual people. Look at them through rose-colored glasses and see that they're cute and endearing!
4. Appreciate each quirk you find. Focus on them and develop gratitude for each and every quirk this person has.

EXPAND YOUR GRATITUDE TO ALL

Do you find it easy to be grateful for someone you love? You probably find it easy to be grateful for at least one or two people in your life; however, if your trouble is in expanding this same gratitude to others, then this is the exercise for you.

Here's how to take your deep and sincere gratitude for one dear person in your life and expand it to encompass everyone:

1. Find a quiet spot to sit and think, and close your eyes.
2. Think of the person you have the most gratitude for. Visualize them clearly in your mind's eye.
3. See your gratitude for them as a glowing light, outlining them. See the gratitude pulse slightly around this person.
4. Now imagine that light expanding and growing. See it envelop another person in your life that you are grateful for.
5. Watch it expand even more to envelop all your most dearly loved friends and family.
6. Take it one step further by expanding it to everyone you know— even those you don't like very much.
7. Finally, visualize the gratitude light expanding so widely that it covers *all* people. Yes, all people, as in all the people in the world. Don't worry; your gratitude is big enough for the task!
8. Sit with this for a few moments, and allow yourself to really feel that gratitude for all people. Commit to carrying that feeling with you after the exercise is over.

VOLUNTEER YOUR TIME AND SERVICES TO A GOOD CAUSE

You might think that volunteering or doing favors for someone and gratitude are a one-way street—that the person on the receiving end feels more gratitude for the giver and that it stops there. Actually, this is not the case! When you volunteer your time and services to a charitable organization or do favors for someone, you often end up feeling more grateful as well.

It's an interesting effect: When you do something good for someone else, you want to like them and believe that it was an altruistic deed on your part. When you feel you did something altruistic, you feel grateful for those who allowed you to engage in this altruistic act.

To take advantage of this effect, consider finding a worthy cause and donating your time and your energy (instead of your money).

If you don't already have one in mind, you have a few options to find one:

* Search online for charitable organizations in your area that might need your time or your skill set.
* Check in with places like hospitals, animal shelters, and churches or other religious organizations to see if you can pitch in.
* Offer to help a family you know is in need or a friend who is going through a rough time.

Whatever your skills or talents, there is always a way to apply them to a good cause! Take some time to help out, and you'll reap the benefits of greater gratitude for those on the receiving end of your efforts.

WRITE
A LOVE LETTER

There's nothing like a love letter to get your gratitude flowing. Taking the time to write out how much you love someone and why you love them is an excellent opportunity to boost your gratitude for them—and likely their gratitude for you as well. It's a win-win!

Follow these steps to pen a heartfelt love letter to someone important to you:

1. Pick the recipient of your love letter. In most cases, this will probably be a spouse or significant other, but don't limit yourself to romantic relationships. You can write a love letter to anyone you love: your best friend, your mom or dad, your child, or anyone else.
2. Take a few minutes to think about all the things you love about this person. Write them down in bullet points if that helps (e.g., "She's an amazing cook" or "He makes me laugh every day").
3. Open the letter with an appropriate greeting, then take your list and turn it into a narrative. Share each reason to love this person in the letter, making sure to use words like "I love you because..." or "This is why I love you..."
4. Close the letter with a heartfelt message of love and gratitude. Thank them for being in your life, and sign it with a flourish.
5. Now all that's left to do is hand it over to your loved one and watch their face as they read it! It will be hard *not* to feel grateful for them.

USE
ACTIVE LISTENING

Active listening is not only a wonderful tool for improving your relationships with those around you—both personal and professional—it's also an effective tool for boosting your gratitude for others.

Here's how it works: You use active listening, you hear more and learn more about your conversation partners, you understand them better and feel more connected to them, and you end up feeling more grateful for them.

To give active listening a try, follow these guidelines:

1. When you talk to someone, make sure to give them your undivided attention.
2. Show them that you are listening and engaged through your words (e.g., providing context-appropriate feedback on what they say) and your body language (e.g., facing toward them, not fiddling or seeming bored).
3. Here's the most important part—actually listen to what they say, rather than formulating your response in your own mind or jumping to conclusions about what they're saying or where they're going with their story.
4. Summarize what you heard and repeat it back to them to ensure you understand what they've said.
5. Respond to them with sincerity and without judgment.

Honor their time and attention through active listening, and you might find that you are better able to understand and accept them as they are, identify and connect with them, and feel grateful for them.

OFFER SINCERE CONGRATULATIONS

If you've ever received some insincere congratulations from someone, you know how discouraging and ultimately meaningless it is. When you get a half-hearted "good for you" in response to an accomplishment or achievement that you are proud of, it can put a damper on your mood, and it certainly won't enhance your gratitude for the person who congratulated you.

On the other hand, when you are offered sincere congratulations for a hard-earned achievement, you not only feel more positive and grateful toward the person who offers it; the person who offers their kind words can also get a boost of gratitude and good feeling.

Here's how to make sure you are giving sincere congratulations on a regular basis:

1. Really listen to people when they tell you about their achievements and accomplishments (if you have trouble with this, try the previous "Use Active Listening" exercise).
2. Imagine how you would feel if you achieved or accomplished whatever the other person has. Visualize the excitement and pleasure you would feel.
3. Apply those feelings to the other person, building your enthusiasm for their good news.
4. Don't hold back! Let your excitement and pleasure show, and make sure you allow your feelings to permeate your words, your tone, and your body language.

PRACTICE METTA BHAVANA (LOVING-KINDNESS MEDITATION)

If you're not familiar with meditation, don't worry! Metta bhavana, or loving-kindness meditation, is not a particularly advanced or difficult form of meditation to practice. However, it does take sustained effort to become comfortable and feel successful with it, so plan on using this exercise on a regular basis if you want to see a real impact.

Follow these steps to practice loving-kindness meditation:

1. Find a comfortable spot and settle in. Close your eyes.
2. Turn your attention to your breath. Feel it, but don't try to control it.
3. Place your hand over your heart and bring to mind loving feelings: kindness, empathy, friendliness, care and concern, and so on. Allow them to grow and spread throughout your chest.
4. Recite some mantras or phrases that will contribute to greater feelings of loving-kindness and gratitude for others. You might try:
   * May I be safe and warm.
   * May I be filled with loving-kindness for others.
   * May I be filled with loving-kindness for myself.
   * May I be at peace.
5. If your mind wanders, gently bring it back to its only purpose right now: thinking about loving-kindness.

When you practice loving-kindness meditation on a regular basis, you open yourself up to greater love and compassion for others (and for yourself too), which naturally leads to a greater sense of gratitude for others.

MAKE SOME
TIME FOR THEM

One of the most effective—and easiest—ways to enhance your gratitude and love for others is to simply make time to spend with them. Time is a precious resource; it's the one thing you can never get back, so choosing to spend it with someone is really the biggest compliment you can give them.

So, to boost your gratitude for others and enhance your connections with your family and friends, commit to spending some quality time with them. It sounds pretty simple, I know. After all, don't you spend tons of time with your partner and your kids already?

We do tend to spend a lot of time with our family and close friends, but that doesn't mean it's quality time. To schedule time with your loved ones that is truly quality time, make sure that time meets these criteria:

* It involves your undivided attention. No checking your phone for texts or emails, no staying preoccupied with projects or deadlines at work, and no leaving the TV on to glance at the basketball scores or the latest news story.
* It's at least a solid hour or two, if not longer. It's possible to have shorter sprints of quality time, but aim high!
* It is spent doing something your loved one(s) enjoys. Spending time together doing only what you like to do is not quality time.

Follow these guidelines to spend quality time with your loved ones, and watch your gratitude grow.

WORK ON
BEING LESS PICKY

Sometimes we can get a little too choosy about the people we spend time with. It's not a bad thing to have standards for your family and friends, but if none of them are living up to your standards, it might be time to work on being less picky and more grateful.

Here's how:

1. Think about someone in your life who has been getting on your nerves. This person should be someone you love but who has some annoying quirks or irritating qualities that drive you crazy. Consider that you still have love for this person, and that you are able to look past their annoying qualities.
2. Face the fact that *you* are irritating to someone else. There are certainly things you do that get on a loved one's nerves, but they still love you anyway.
3. Realize that everyone has their quirks and flaws, but that this doesn't stop us from loving one another. Having a few irritating qualities is no reason to shut them out of your life. If you look close enough, you're sure to find at least one reason to be grateful for everyone you know.
4. Think about someone you have recently shunned or shut out due to something that seems small or insignificant now, and invite them out for coffee or lunch.

Learning to accept and appreciate people for who they are is one of the best ways to enhance your gratitude for others—even those who make you want to tear your hair out!

CREATE ONE JOURNAL ENTRY
FOR EACH LOVED ONE

This exercise is based on the powerful potential of journaling. If you haven't started journaling, see the "Start a Gratitude Journal" exercise in Chapter 4.

Once you have your journal or notebook at the ready, prepare yourself for the exercise by thinking of the most significant people in your life; this will probably include your spouse or significant other, your children, your parents, your siblings, and/or your closest friends. Choose the five or six who are *most* important to you and write each name at the top of its own page in your journal.

Take a few minutes to complete a journal entry for each loved one. Just freewrite about why you are grateful for each person, create a bulleted list of reasons why you love them, or even address them in your journal entry to tell them why you are grateful for them. The entries don't have to be very long; they just need to be authentic and from the heart.

This exercise will not only help you be more grateful for those five or six people in particular; it will also help you adopt a perspective that looks for the good in others rather than seeing the worst. This perspective will contribute to feeling more gratitude for others overall.

GIVE
A SMALL GIFT

Gifts are the best, aren't they? They're fun to give and fun to receive, and they're an excellent way to show someone you care about them.

It's easy to feel grateful when someone buys you a gift, but it's just as easy to boost your gratitude when you buy others a gift as well. To take advantage of this opportunity to enhance your gratitude for others, give them a small gift.

It doesn't have to be much, and it doesn't even have to cost anything. Here are some cheap or free options for small gifts:

* A framed photo of the two of you.
* A bunch of wildflowers you gathered or flowers you cut from your backyard.
* A homemade treat, like a cake or cookies.
* Any other crafty homemade item, like jewelry, a keepsake box, or a small woodworking project.
* A keychain, necklace, or other trinket that relates to something they love, like their favorite TV show or book series.
* A small gift card to their favorite coffee shop, with just enough to get them their favorite drink for a day or two.

Give your loved one a small gift, with no expectations of anything in return, and you'll enjoy a boost to your gratitude for him or her.

GIVE
A GENUINE COMPLIMENT

You know how it feels to get a really nice compliment—one that's meaningful and thoughtful, not just a social nicety or something people say to be polite. It feels great! When you receive a genuine, sincere compliment, you not only get those nice, warm fuzzy feelings; you also tend to feel more grateful to the compliment giver and more connected to them.

Put the power of compliments to good use by giving someone else an authentic compliment. Here's what to do:

1. Be on the lookout for something you really admire about someone, whether it's a personality trait, a fashion choice, or an impressive accomplishment.
2. Take note of what it is you admire. Is it the person's work ethic? Their kindness? Their skill in art or music? Figure out exactly what it is you admire.
3. Share it with this person! Tell them what you admire and why, and be sincere and authentic when you do it. Keep your body language and tone friendly and open to help show your sincerity.

Sharing your admiration for someone else will make you feel those warm fuzzy feelings too, and will put you on the path to being more positive toward and grateful for others.

ENCOURAGE
GRATITUDE IN OTHERS

Why are there groups dedicated to reaching goals (e.g., weight loss groups, public speaking groups, groups for would-be entrepreneurs)?

Because you are often more effective in meeting your goals when you are with others interested in the same goals, and you are all supporting and encouraging each other to succeed. Of course, lots of people succeed in reaching their goals when they go it alone, but generally it's easier to stay inspired and motivated with some buddies who share our goals.

The goal of cultivating greater gratitude is no exception to this rule; if your goal is to be more grateful in general and more grateful for other people in particular, there's no better way to pursue it than to involve others in your efforts.

Invite your friends and family to join you in your gratitude exercises. Show them how to journal for gratitude, how to find gratitude in silent reflection or in observing nature, and how to change up their perspective to find the good all around them. Attend a yoga class with them and set a gratitude intention. The possibilities for involving your loved ones in your pursuit of greater gratitude are endless!

Be sure to give your friends and family your sincere thanks for participating in any gratitude activities with you and encourage them to share their gratitude with others as well.

PLAN A
SPECIAL DATE

When you want to show someone you love them or tell them how much they mean to you, what do you do? You might buy them gifts, do an act of service (like taking care of something they are dreading), or simply tell them how you feel, but one of the most popular ways to show you care is to take someone on a special date or outing.

Although the word *date* brings to mind a boyfriend/girlfriend or a spouse, you don't need to keep this exercise to romantic partners. You can take anyone you love out for a date: your child, your mom or dad, your best friend, your grandchild—the list is endless.

Keep these guidelines in mind as you plan your special date or outing with your loved one:

* Make sure to invite your loved one and get the date on their calendar so you're safe to plan things during that time slot.
* Consider your loved one's favorite things to do or things on their wish list, like eating at a high-end restaurant, taking a hot-air balloon ride, going for a scenic drive, going on a picnic, or attending a concert.
* Choose something you and your loved one will both enjoy doing and plan the whole afternoon or evening around it.

Allow thoughts of your loved one's joy at being taken on such a fun date to fill your mind, and turn that joy into gratitude for them.

CHAPTER 4

EXERCISES TO CULTIVATE GRATITUDE FOR YOUR PAST AND PRESENT

We often find it difficult to be grateful for our past, especially if we've endured trauma and pain. Many of us may also find it difficult to appreciate our present, due to anxiety or simply our many day-to-day stressors. This chapter will provide you with twenty-five ways to work around that anxiety and stress. The exercises here will teach you how to understand your past, let go of your past, make peace with your past, appreciate your present, and be thankful for what you have. You will learn how to find the silver lining, identify lessons learned from your past, and look to the future with excitement and gratitude.

MEDITATE
ON YOUR PAST

Meditation can have amazing benefits for both your physical and mental health. It can be used to calm, soothe, and center you, all of which contribute to a better mental state.

With a few tweaks, it can also be used to cultivate gratitude for your past and your present.

To give it a try, follow these steps:

1. Find a quiet and comfortable spot to sit and close your eyes.
2. Allow your breath to come and go naturally—don't try to force it into any certain rhythm or pattern.
3. Focus on how it feels to breathe in and out, your chest rising and falling as your lungs alternately fill with air and empty themselves.
4. When you feel centered and focused, turn your attention to your past. Think about the defining moments that brought you to where you are today. See them in isolation, and connect them to the present you.
5. For any moments that come with guilt, anger, shame, sadness, or any other negative emotion, cut the string that holds these feelings to that moment. With your next breath, imagine them floating away.
6. Practice gratitude for each defining moment of your past and appreciate it for getting you to where you are now.
7. Return your focus to your breath and slowly return to the present.

This might feel difficult or unnatural at first, since meditation is so often geared toward letting go of the past, but remember not to throw out the good with the bad.

HAVE A CONVERSATION WITH YOUR PAST SELF

You've probably seen one of those movies where, through the magic of time travel or some supernatural force, a character is able to share a quick message with his or her past self.

Unfortunately, we do not have the technology necessary for such a conversation! What we do have is the ability to think back on our old selves and connect them to our present self.

When you have a little spare time and you're feeling centered and ready, think back to an important moment in your life. It should be at least a few years past and during a time of indecision, confusion, or stress. Visualize this version of yourself in detail—what is this version dealing with in this moment?

Once you have a clear image in mind, think about what you want to tell this former version of you. Consider what would have pleased that version to know about the future; for instance, you may want to reassure your former self that they are making a good decision that will positively affect events to come.

After you share your message with your former self, think about how you got from there to here. Send some gratitude toward your past self, and extend it to your current self as well. Be thankful for what you've experienced, because it brought you to where you are now.

DRAW
A TIME LINE

One of the most effective ways to feel grateful for your past is to see it all outlined. You may have trouble feeling grateful for something bad that happened in the past, but when you see it in context, you might feel differently.

Here's how to create your own personal time line:

1. Draw a straight line. At the far right end, write "now." At the far left end, write "my birth." Those are the easy ones!
2. Now for the more difficult ones. Imagine you have to make a list of the five most important or significant moments, decisions, or events in your life. What would make the list? Summer camp as a child? Going off to college, perhaps? Maybe getting married, starting your current job, or the birth of your first child.
3. For each significant moment or event, find the right place for it on the time line and label it.
4. Once you have written and labeled all five moments on your time line, see if you can think of any more to add.
5. When you're finished adding events, look over your time line. Think about how each of those events shaped who you are today, and how they made future events possible.
6. Think about how easy it would have been for even one of those events to go a different way. Cultivate a sense of gratitude for each of these events, even if they were difficult or traumatic at the time.

THANK
YOUR PAST SELF

To really feel grateful for your past, it helps to be as personal as possible. A good way to do this is to visualize your past self and say "thank you" directly to yourself.

Follow these steps to give this exercise a try:

1. Choose a past version of yourself. Think of a moment when you made a decision you are proud of or achieved something impressive.
2. Visualize this past version of yourself in as much detail as possible. If you can remember what you were wearing, where you were at a significant moment, who you were with, and so on, all the better.
3. See this past version of yourself walking, talking, and going about the day. In other words, see yourself "in motion" to make it feel as real as possible.
4. Reach out to this past version of you and share your gratitude with them for what they did. Don't just visualize saying "thanks" and walking away; tell your past self exactly what you are grateful for and why. For example, you might say, "Thank you so much for persevering in your math classes. I know they were really difficult at the time, but they led to an amazing career that would not have been possible without those classes."
5. Feel the warmth in your chest and embrace the feeling of gratitude you have cultivated for yourself. Allow yourself to sink into it and enjoy it for a minute or two.

MAKE A LIST OF REASONS TO BE PROUD OF "PAST YOU"

If you have trouble thanking your past self or feeling grateful for the things you have done in the past, this exercise can help you get around that.

To encourage pride in your past self, take out your journal or some scratch paper and prepare to make a list. You might write something like, "Why I Should Be Proud of Me" at the top.

Think back to your biggest accomplishments. Consider what you have achieved that not everyone has—like graduating from high school, getting a great job offer, running a half-marathon, graduating with an advanced degree, or nailing a tough project at work.

Note each of these achievements and accomplishments on your list. Think of your earliest successes and of those from just a month or so ago.

When you finish your list, take a few minutes to read through it. As you read, try to be as objective as possible. Imagine that this past version of yourself is someone else, and think of how proud you would be if that was your child or someone you loved. Encourage a sense of pride in this individual, then bring it back by reminding yourself that it was all you!

Allow yourself to feel pride in the things you have accomplished, and thank yourself for working as hard as you have to accomplish them.

CONSIDER WHAT YOU KNOW AND WHY YOU KNOW IT

We aren't always aware of exactly how and where we picked up the skills and knowledge we have now. Sometimes we may just assume we've always had them!

If your aim is to incorporate more gratitude into your life, then it's important to put your past and present into perspective; instead of giving no thought to how you gained the tools and resources you have now, this exercise will encourage you to be aware of how it all happened.

Think about all the special skills, knowledge, and tools you have now. Include both work-related and personal skills, knowledge, and tools. You can make a list if that helps.

Pick a few of the most important ones, or the ones you use most often.

For each of these skills, write a sentence or two about how you gained it. For example, you might write: "I gained my self-confidence after that awful breakup when I was twenty-two. It was a terrible period of my life that taught me what I'm capable of."

Once you've identified a source for each of your skills, read through what you've written and express your gratitude for the path that led you to each one. Say it out loud to make it more impactful. For example, you could say, "I'm so grateful I went through such a nasty breakup early in my twenties. It helped me to gain the self-confidence I needed to avoid some major mistakes later down the road."

CHAT WITH A PARENT ABOUT YOUR CHILDHOOD

If you have trouble thinking about the good parts of your past or feeling grateful for your childhood, this exercise will help you. Remembering the good parts of your childhood is an excellent way to cultivate more gratitude for your past, and talking to your parents about your childhood is a great way to remember the good parts of your childhood!

Call up your mom or dad to arrange a dinner or some other get-together in the near future. If you live too far from your parents to meet in person, see if you can video chat.

When you talk to your parent or parents, ask them these questions to give your memory a little boost:

* When was I happiest as a child?
* What were my favorite things to do when I was young?
* What was your favorite moment with me as a kid?
* What did we love to do together?
* Where did I love to go when I was young?

These questions are sure to prompt them into a walk down memory lane! Walk with them and try to remember the stories they tell about you. Revel in the experience and make sure to be grateful for all the good times you had as a child.

BRING THE PAST INTO THE PRESENT WITH YOUR CHILDREN

If you don't have a parent around to chat with about your childhood (see the previous exercise), you can always inject some gratitude into your life by talking with your children about your childhood. You might even get a chance to relive some of the best parts of your childhood with them.

If you have very young children, you'll need to keep them engaged with funny or exciting stories about when you were a kid. If your children are older, you'll be able to share more meaningful stories with them.

Tell them about some of your favorite memories and the best experiences you had as a child. Focus on the funny memories, the thrilling moments, and the experiences that are most imprinted in your memory.

Follow these guidelines for sharing:

* Be honest. Make sure you're not stretching the truth or editing out any important moments because they're embarrassing or include bad behavior on your part.
* However, you don't have to share every single thing with your kids; use your judgment to share only age-appropriate memories with them.
* Tell your kids that you love making memories like this with them as well, and ask them about their favorite memories.

Reliving the best parts of your past is a great way to feel more gratitude for your past, and sharing with your children is one of the best ways to do that.

FLIP THROUGH
OLD PHOTOS

If telling stories isn't really your thing or you tend to forget important details when talking about your past, try using a stack of old photos to guide your reminiscing.

Flipping through your old photos helps you to remember all the good times, all the bad times, and all the other experiences that led you to where you are today.

So, to give yourself a boost of gratitude for your past and present, find a stack of pictures or an album you haven't looked at in a while and set aside some time to leaf through the pages.

As your gaze falls on each photo, take a few moments to put yourself back in that moment. Whether you took the photo, star in the photo, or are not in the photo at all, think about your circumstances when the picture was taken—where you were, who you were with, how old you were, what you were doing, and what was going on in your head at that moment.

If you're flipping through photos with a friend or loved one, narrate these facts out loud to them, highlighting anything particularly interesting or noteworthy.

Make the connection between who you were at that point and who you are now, and give a little silent prayer or expression of thanks for the experiences that led you to where you are now.

FOCUS ON
THE POSITIVE

It's a good idea to reflect on *all* of your past—the positive and the negative. That's how you get perspective, take stock, and formulate the lessons you learned for yourself.

However, for the purposes of developing greater gratitude for your past and present, it can be especially effective to focus only on the positive for a bit.

Rather than explicitly linking your past experiences with your current reality, this exercise simply requires you to think about the good old times and spend a few moments appreciating them.

Here's what to do:

1. Grab a journal or notebook to organize your thoughts and get things down on paper.
2. List the five most positive memories you have. These memories can come from any point in time from your earliest memory to a few minutes ago. You'll probably gravitate to the big ones (e.g., graduating from college, getting married, birth of a child), but don't hesitate to use the smaller moments too!
3. Continue listing positive memories until you have a whole page full of them, or until your hand is too cramped up to write anymore!
4. Read through this list of the best things that have happened to you and give thanks—to the universe, to God, to yourself, or to anyone or anything else you choose.

Use this list of positive memories to keep yourself grateful for everything you've experienced.

LOOK TO
THE FUTURE

It sounds counterintuitive, but one good way to appreciate everything behind you and around you now is to look into your future. If your expected future is a positive one, it's easy to cultivate gratitude for where you are today and where you've been.

Here's how to look to the future to boost your gratitude for the past and present:

1. Find a quiet spot to sit and think without interruption. Get comfortable and close your eyes.
2. Imagine your future on your current course. If you feel you're a bit off course right now, imagine your future with the tweaks you need to make to get back to where you want to be.
3. Visualize this future in detail. Who are you with? What are you doing? Where are you living? What are your hobbies? And most important, how have *you* changed for the better?
4. When you have a good image of this potential future and have some details in mind, open your eyes and grab some paper and something to write with. Write down where you are now in terms of these details, and where you are in your vision of the future.
5. Now that you have two endpoints, think about how they connect. Think about the steps that need to be taken to get from "here" to "there."
6. Allow yourself to feel gratitude for where you are now and for how you got here, since it is one of the many steps that will take you to your desired future.

SET AND CELEBRATE
RETROACTIVE GOALS

This exercise requires some mental gymnastics, but it can be extremely effective. Think about big things you have accomplished over the past few months or years and do some retroactive goal-setting: looking back, setting goals for the things you have *already* done, and checking them off your mental to-do list.

If this sounds like cheating on your goals, I get it! It does feel a little odd, but it can be really effective in helping you cultivate gratitude for what you have already done and what you already have.

Here's how to do it:

1. Grab some paper and a pen and write down at least three of the biggest things you have accomplished in the last year or so. For example, did you get a new job with a better salary? Or maybe you lost ten pounds or got engaged? Be creative if you need to be; just make sure you write down at least three accomplishments that you are proud of and happy about.
2. Now here's where you need to use some imagination: Take yourself back in time to about a year ago, before you accomplished any of these things. Really put yourself in "past you's" shoes.
3. Write down that you are setting these three goals for yourself. Go into detail if you wish.
4. Here's the fun part—cross them off your list and celebrate them! Act like they just happened, and feel the pride and gratitude for your circumstances that you felt at each event.

COUNT YOUR BLESSINGS
WHEN YOU WAKE UP

Start your day on the right side of the bed by counting your blessings the moment you wake up. Morning may not be your favorite time, but it's a great time to practice a little gratitude and set yourself up for a good day.

The moment you wake up, as soon as you turn off your alarm, think of at least five or six things you're grateful for right now. If you can, try to practice this exercise before you even open your eyes.

When you count your blessings at such a unique and vulnerable time, you often come up with some interesting, silly, and profound blessings. For example, you might be immediately grateful that it's summer because it's light out when you wake up, rather than dark and dreary. You might find yourself being thankful that you live just down the street from your favorite coffee shop, or perhaps you'll be filled with love and thankfulness for your significant other lying beside you in bed.

Whatever it is you're grateful for in the morning, you can be sure that it's honest and authentically you.

If you're the kind of person who wakes with little idea of your plans for the day—or even what your own name is—you might want to set a reminder on your phone or just put a sticky note where you'll see it right away.

COUNT YOUR BLESSINGS
WHEN YOU GO TO BED

Of course, you can count your blessings at any time of day, and it's a good idea to go to bed on the "right side" as well. Going to bed in the right mood is a commonly given piece of advice and just an all-around good idea.

Use the opportunity to practice gratitude and put yourself in a good mood for the night!

When you've done all your nightly rituals—brushed your teeth, washed your face, changed into your pajamas—hop into bed and finish up any last things you need to do, like plugging in your phone, kissing your significant other good night, and turning out the light.

Now, when you're just about ready to sleep, take a few minutes to count your blessings. Think of at least five things that are a blessing in your life right now: anything from the monumental (your sense of meaning in your work and purpose in your life) to the small and mundane (making it to ten punches on your punch card for the sandwich shop).

Count your blessings before you go to bed to make sure you sleep a little easier, dream a little more joyfully, and wake a little more positively.

START A
GRATITUDE JOURNAL

Journaling is an effective tool for addressing many common complaints and problems; it can help you learn to be more expressive, help you understand your past, encourage you to reflect and introspect, and more.

As you might have guessed, it's also a great way to develop and maintain a healthy gratitude practice.

If you don't already have one, go out and buy a notebook or journal to use in your daily gratitude practice, and try to keep it strictly for that purpose—no grocery lists or to-dos in these pages!

To get started with your gratitude journal, try this first entry:

1. Put your commitment to practice gratitude in words, and be specific. Specify that you are aiming for, say, five minutes of writing each evening.
2. Write down *why* you are committing to this practice. What do you hope to get out of it? What do you expect it will do for you?
3. Kick off your journaling by freewriting about what you are grateful for, right here and now, in this very moment. Don't make a numbered list or use bullet points, and don't worry about proper grammar or spelling, just write whatever comes to mind. For example, you might find yourself writing something like, "I'm so grateful that I have the ability to write because not everyone does and not everyone has a warm and comfortable space to write in, let alone the money to buy a journal or even to buy food. I'm so lucky."

GET OUT AND
TRY SOMETHING NEW

Trying new things is an effective way to work toward many goals and desires, including coming out of your shell, getting motivated, finding inspiration, or increasing your confidence. In addition to all of these potential benefits, it can also help you boost your gratitude for yourself, your present, and your future.

When you try something novel—especially if it's challenging, fun, and/or totally unfamiliar to you—you activate new pathways in the brain. These new pathways open you up to other ways of thinking and seeing the world, and that opens you up to being more grateful for where you are, how you got here, and where you'll go.

So, if you want to cultivate greater gratitude, give something new a try! Here are a few examples, although this list is by no means comprehensive:

* A physical activity, like running, a fitness class, or weight lifting.
* An outdoor activity, like hiking, birdwatching, skiing, or kayaking.
* A group activity, like a book club, a knitting group, or a board game group.
* A skill-based activity, like painting, woodworking, or archery.

Getting out of your comfort zone and trying something new will remind you that you *can* do something new—after all, everything was new to you at one point. It will also remind you of the endless potential of your future. Take those reminders and channel them into greater gratitude for what you've done, what you're doing, and what you will do.

PRACTICE MINDFULNESS ON A REGULAR BASIS

Mindfulness is a cure for many common ailments; it can help you increase your self-awareness and your awareness in general, enhance your sense of peace and ability to remain calm, and even make you happier. In addition to these benefits, practicing regular mindfulness can also help you feel more gratitude for the present.

Here's a quick introduction to mindfulness practice:

1. Find a comfortable spot, relax, and close your eyes.
2. Focus on your breath, without trying to control it. Pay attention to the way it feels to inhale and exhale, and feel your chest rise and fall.
3. Turn your attention to your body. Think about how your body feels in your current position and notice the sensations in your muscles.
4. Now pay attention to your mind. Allow your thoughts to drift through your mind instead of latching on to any of them. Observe them without judgment and let them go.
5. If your mind wanders, gently bring it back to nonjudgmental observation.
6. When you're ready, slowly open your eyes and bring your awareness to your environment. Commit to carrying your mindfulness with you throughout the day.

To practice mindfulness on a regular basis, be sure to do three things:

1. Schedule time for it; don't just assume it will happen on its own.
2. Set a time goal for yourself; five minutes is fine to start with, but you may want to increase it as you get better at it.
3. Try practicing mindfulness in different contexts and at different times.

MAKE PEACE
WITH THE PAST

Making peace with the more traumatic or negative parts of your past is tough, but it's one of the best things you can do to enhance your gratitude for the present and move forward with more gratitude in the future.

Here's a five-step process that will help you make peace with your past:

1. Face the difficult memories in your past. Trying to keep them buried won't work, so you might as well bring them to the surface now. Put your thoughts and feelings down on paper.
2. Accept that this is your past. It's hard to accept some of the bad things that happened to you, but it's essential for making peace.
3. Think about any silver linings that came out of your trauma or troubles. Did you learn important lessons or gain useful coping skills? Write them down.
4. If any of your wounds were inflicted by a certain person or people you still find hard to forgive, realize that any recognition, apology, or amends from them have no bearing on your ability to heal. It's nice if you get those things, but don't expect them, and know that you don't need them.
5. Forgive yourself and forgive those who hurt you. You don't need to believe that what they did was okay, nor do you need to feel warm and fuzzy toward them, but the only person you're hurting by refusing to forgive is yourself.

GIVE THANKS FOR THE MISTAKES YOU HAVE MADE

It sounds like a strange idea, doesn't it? Why would you be thankful for making mistakes? You hate making mistakes, and they often have unpleasant consequences.

Although you may not like making mistakes, it's an inevitable part of life. You can't escape it—and you shouldn't want to. Your most impactful lessons can come from the fallout of making mistakes.

Think of it this way: You wouldn't be who you are today without the mistakes you made. If you've been working on your self-gratitude, then you'll realize that some of those mistakes were blessings in disguise!

To cultivate a sense of gratitude for the mistakes under your belt, try these steps:

1. Think of your three or four biggest mistakes; these should be the really impactful ones, like forgetting an extremely important appointment or missing out on a great opportunity.
2. Think of at least one lesson you learned from each mistake. For example, you may have learned the importance of proper scheduling and the use of notifications and alarms if you missed something important.
3. Remind yourself of the value of these lessons you learned and skills you gained. Be thankful for these positive outcomes from a negative situation.

Going forward, remember to go easy on yourself when you make mistakes, and be sure to look for the silver lining!

ALLOW YOURSELF
TO WANT MORE

Many people find that the one thing that gets in the way of enjoying what they have and feeling grateful for where they are right now is an oft-praised trait in our society: ambition. The desire to succeed and the drive to achieve have resulted in amazing accomplishments and brought about life-changing innovations; however, those who experience ambition may find it difficult to be thankful for what they have.

Luckily, ambition and gratitude for the present are not mutually exclusive! Try this exercise to feel grateful for what you have while allowing yourself to want more.

The key lies in managing your "wants." It's okay to want things, like a promotion, a better salary, or more success, especially when those are things you are actively working toward. What's not so healthy is wanting everything, all of your desires and goals and wishes, and wanting them *right now.*

Being able to acknowledge what you have right now, understand what you're working toward, and recognize if there's anything you want that you aren't willing to work for is a good way to maintain a healthy sense of gratitude for what you have while avoiding any potential guilt for wanting more.

Tell yourself it's okay to strive for more; just be sure to cultivate gratitude for what you already have first!

SPEND SOME TIME DAYDREAMING

Daydreaming isn't just a time-waster; it can actually be a healthy mental activity! Allowing yourself to drift into the dreamworld of broad daylight can boost your imagination and give your brain the break it needs to process whatever's going on in your life right now.

Plus, daydreams tend toward the positive, meaning that daydreaming will allow you to explore the good things in your life. Daydreams involving others are particularly positive and can actually boost your connection—even when the interaction is only in your head! All this positivity in your daydreams will lead you to feel even more gratitude for your present.

To harness the gratitude benefits of daydreaming, follow these simple steps:

1. Find somewhere comfortable to sit, preferably with a good view out the window or looking out into nature. Set an alarm for ten or fifteen minutes.
2. Look outside or around you and find anything that catches your eye or interests you.
3. Allow your mind to simply wander based on this one interesting thing; for example, if you see something that reminds you of a painting you like, let your mind wander to the painting, then other similar paintings, then artists you like, etc. Don't try to route it in any certain direction, just allow it to go where it will.
4. Once the alarm goes off, stop and think about all the positive things that came to mind. Cultivate gratitude for the positive things in your life and feel grateful for your present.

GIVE THANKS FOR EACH OF YOUR MEALS TODAY

You are probably familiar with the concept of giving thanks for your food. Cultures around the world give thanks to a variety of gods, deities, forces, or the universe itself, but the common theme among all of them is expressing gratitude for what you have.

To boost your gratitude for your present, try giving thanks for not one but *all* of your meals today. You can do it out loud or privately to yourself; say a quick "thanks" or make a more prolonged expression of gratitude. The choice is yours!

If you're not familiar with giving thanks for your meal, here's a good secular option:

1. When you sit down to eat, think about the journey your food had to take to get to you today. Think about each of the ingredients being grown, raised, or gathered, and packaged and distributed across the state, the country, or even the world.
2. Think of all the people who were involved in this process: the farmers, the laborers, the packagers and quality checkers, the shippers and distributors, and your local grocers and their employees.
3. Consider how much time and effort went into making this meal for you. Think about how unthinkable this would have been even a couple hundred years ago.
4. Cultivate gratitude for your food—and your ability to buy the food, which not everyone has—and offer it up to everyone involved in the process.

BE PRESENT
AT WORK

Although drifting off to daydream land is tempting (and not so bad—see the earlier exercise, "Spend Some Time Daydreaming"), the negative consequences will probably outweigh the benefits if you do it when you're at work.

Being present at work is not only a good way to nurture your career and grow your skills; it's also a good way to boost your gratitude for where you are in life right now.

Here's how to be more present at work:

* Practice mindfulness before and during work—just keep it to around five minutes when you're on the job.
* Gently bring your mind back to the task at hand when it begins to wander.
* Set yourself goals that are independent of your manager's wishes or the formal goals HR might set for you.
* Find a sense of pride and meaning in what you do; be aware of how you contribute to the team, the organization, and the community.

People who stay focused and on task at work are more likely to enjoy their job and to perform well in their role. They also open themselves up to more gratitude for their present and the past that qualified them to be where they are now. So what are you waiting for? It's worth a shot!

PICK A
GRATITUDE TRIGGER

A trigger is any kind of stimulus that sets off a certain reaction, often a flashback or memory. A negative trigger is associated with post-traumatic stress disorder or other trauma-inflicted wounds and can bring up all the painful memories and difficult feelings when you see, hear, or even smell it.

However, a trigger doesn't have to be something dark and depressing—you can create a happy trigger for yourself! Instead of leading to traumatic thoughts and emotions, this trigger will lead to gratitude for the present.

Sound interesting? Good! Here's what to do:

1. Find any object that you will see regularly throughout your day—but maybe not *too* regularly. It could be the clock in your kitchen, a motivational poster in the break room at work, or even a small object that you carry with you.
2. Every time you see this object (or feel it, if it's something you carry with you), use it as a reminder to be grateful for this exact moment. Let it trigger your gratitude for where you are, what you are doing, and who you are with.
3. Decide on a mini-gratitude practice, affirmations, or mantra to exercise or repeat when you encounter your gratitude trigger. You might say something like, "I am grateful for the present and thankful for this moment."

Practice this exercise enough and you will notice that the gratitude trigger starts to trigger gratitude on its own, without any effort on your part!

ACCEPT
THE GIFT OF LIFE

I know, the title of this exercise may seem broad and a little vague—after all, how do you accept the gift of life, and what will that do for you? What it can do for you is significantly increase your gratitude for your past, present, and future!

To accept life as the wonderful, amazing gift that it is, try these steps:

1. Imagine that you were never born. It's impossible, right? What was there before you were born? What is there after? A lot of us have ideas, but we don't know for sure.

2. Think about all the good things you would have missed if you had never been born. Sure, you would have avoided all your pain, but you would have missed out on all the beauty you have experienced too.

3. See all the beauty that has touched your life as the miraculous gift it is. Embrace the gift, whoever or whatever gave it to you, and know that it is truly the greatest gift any of us will ever receive.

4. Cultivate a profound sense of gratitude for this gift! Let it permeate your perspective and color your view on everything that happens in your life. You will probably find that the bad stuff isn't quite so bad anymore, and that it's easier than ever to feel gratitude for your past, present, and future.

CHAPTER 5

EXERCISES TO CULTIVATE GRATITUDE FOR YOUR SURROUNDINGS

We so often forget to appreciate what is around us. When we stop and look, we usually find that our environment is wondrous and full of things to experience and enjoy. This chapter will help you practice gratitude for everything around you, through cultivating a gratitude practice on the go, finding things to love in your current circumstances, moving to new and exciting circumstances, creating gratitude statements, and making small changes that will have a big impact on your life. You'll find that the more you practice gratitude for your surroundings, the more grateful you will be for all things in your life, and the more positive your general outlook will be.

FIND THREE THINGS NEAR YOU TO BE GRATEFUL FOR

If you need an instant pick-me-up injection of gratitude, this is a great exercise for you. All you need is a few minutes to spare and some eyes to see with!

Stop what you're doing, close your eyes, and take a deep breath. Now take another deep breath. And one more. Try to empty your mind of any worries or concerns that were just filling it.

Now let your eyelids flutter open. Look at your surroundings with a fresh set of eyes and an open mind. Find three things around you that you are grateful for. These three things should be fairly close to you. If you are inside, they should be in the room you are in; if you are outside, they should be within twenty feet or so.

Try to find things that aren't too generic or broad, like "sunshine" or "air to breathe." Look for things that you may not notice most of the time, or things you might take for granted.

When you spot one, tell yourself why you are grateful to this object, and—if it doesn't feel too awkward—tell the object you are grateful for it.

For example, you might pick a pillow with a sham that your grandmother embroidered for you; tell it you are grateful for it because it brightens up the room and reminds you of your beloved grandmother.

Do this for each object, and you'll realize that you suddenly have a sunnier outlook!

START A "MOBILE" GRATITUDE PRACTICE

We often get into habits and find it hard to get out of them. Even good habits can sometimes hinder you if they're too constrained or restricted.

One good example is a gratitude practice. Lots of people create a gratitude practice that assumes they are at home, in a quiet place, and able to stop what they are doing and focus only on gratitude. That's a great way to practice gratitude, but if you want to start a practice that is truly embedded in your life, you've got to get mobile!

A mobile gratitude practice is one that can be practiced anywhere, anytime, in any situation. It doesn't require you to close your eyes, have absolute silence, or narrow your focus.

Instead, it places gratitude in your context. It incorporates the people and things around you into your practice and ultimately enhances your gratitude. It's something you can do at home, in the car, at the office, at your kids' soccer game, or in your doctor's waiting room.

To start your own practice, all you need to do is get into the habit of noticing things you are grateful for and expressing that gratitude (either to yourself or out loud) in the moment. For example, you might be in line at a coffee shop and catch a whiff of some really excellent coffee, and embrace gratitude for the coffee, the baristas, and the coffee shop in general.

Take your gratitude on the go for a truly embedded practice!

FIND THINGS TO LOVE
ABOUT YOUR TOWN/CITY

Hating on the place you live—it's a common thing to do, but it's a habit that is ultimately unhelpful. You have probably heard such complaints from people you grew up with, or you may have even done it yourself.

Teenagers and young adults often get pulled into this unintentional practice—you often hear them say things like, "This town sucks" or "There's nothing to do here" or "[My city] is so boring!"

To counteract this unhelpful habit, practice finding things to love about your hometown or the city you are currently living or working in. If this requires you to go out and experience more of the town, that's an added bonus!

To get started, try these ideas:

* If you live in a walkable area, walk a different route that takes you by places you've never been before. Keep an eye out for good restaurants, movie theaters, or interesting shops.
* Check out your town's "center," whether that's a town commons, a park, an ice-skating rink, and so on.
* Close your eyes and point to a spot on the map of your town, and go there!

Broaden your horizons, keep your eyes peeled for the good things around you, and stay open-minded to new places, people, and ideas, and you'll be surprised at how many things you find to love about your town.

USE A
GRATITUDE REMINDER

If you're like most people, you might be totally committed to the idea of doing something but end up scolding yourself at the end of the day because you forgot to do it! Our lives are so packed with activities and appointments that it's totally understandable when something falls through the cracks.

To make sure practicing gratitude doesn't fall through the cracks, here's a handy trick: Set a gratitude reminder on your phone.

You can set it for whatever time works for you, whether that's first thing in the morning, at lunchtime, right after you get home, or just before bed. When the reminder pops up on your phone, take just five minutes—or even two minutes, if you're really low on time—to think about what you are grateful for today.

It could be something small, like the barista getting your coffee *just* right this morning, or something bigger, like the job that allows you to pay your bills.

Setting a reminder will make you much more likely to find the time to be grateful. Just make sure you don't dismiss the reminder before you actually engage in your gratitude practice—that's a good way to forget.

CREATE A GRATITUDE STATEMENT FOR WORK

If you have trouble being grateful for your surroundings at work, this exercise is a good choice. It may be that your workplace isn't so bad—you just need a prompt to get yourself in a grateful frame of mind!

A gratitude statement is like a mantra or a motto, something you can pull out whenever you're distracted or turned away from gratitude. As you might imagine, such statements can be very effective at work, where you are surrounded by distractions, stressors, irritations, and challenges.

Although the work environment makes it more difficult to practice gratitude, it also makes it one of the best times to work on your practice!

To set yourself up for success in practicing gratitude at work, create your gratitude work statement with the following steps:

1. Think about what you do at work—not just your job title but the actual work you engage in on a daily basis.
2. Think about the point of all you do; what is the outcome of your work? What is the end result of your daily efforts?
3. Connect the two in a gratitude statement. Put it in this format: "I am grateful that I am able to [work you do] because it results in [outcome of your work]."
4. Remind yourself of this statement throughout your workday to stay appreciative of where you are and what you're doing. If you need help remembering it, write it down and leave it somewhere you will see it often.

GIVE SOMEONE
A POSITIVE TOUR

If you've ever played host to a guest from out of town, you know it can be a pretty fun experience! It's nice to get a chance to share the best things around you with others. You might find that you actually frame things in the best way possible to make your town seem even more appealing!

To boost your gratitude for your surroundings, try giving someone you know a "positive tour." This person could be someone who is new to the area or just an amenable friend or family member who is willing to take your tour.

Here's how to give the tour:

1. Invite your tourist to join you and explain what kind of tour you'll be giving them.
2. Lead them around your town, your area, your neighborhood, or even just your house, pointing out important and noteworthy things as you go.
3. Make sure that each important and noteworthy thing you point out is a good thing, and try to give the tour the most positive skew you can. Give your friend or family member the tour as if you're trying to convince them to vacation here or move here; in other words, try to be as persuasive and positive as possible!

That positivity will rub off on you and make it easy to feel grateful for where you live.

FIND SOMETHING THAT MAKES YOU SMILE

This is a pretty simple exercise—one that you can do without any tools, preparation, or props. It's also pretty quick, making it an ideal choice for someone who struggles to find the time to practice gratitude. All you need is your eyes to see and a mouth to smile!

Here's the exercise:

1. Stop what you're doing, close your eyes, and take a couple of centering breaths. Breathe in deeply through your nose, filling your lungs, and then exhale it all out. Repeat until you feel a little calmer and more centered.
2. Open your eyes and look around you. Find just one happy thing, or a thing that makes you smile. It could be something that strikes an idea or brings up a memory, or something that is simply pleasing to look at.
3. Focus on this object. Consider what it is about this object that makes you smile, and dwell on that for a moment.
4. Smile! Let your joy and appreciation of this object shine out in a smile. Don't worry who is around or what people will think of you grinning like a maniac—you probably look happy and friendly, not weird or crazy!

Find one thing that makes you smile, and you'll find that it's not so hard to develop gratitude for all things around you.

MAKE
A SMALL CHANGE

Sometimes the tiniest of changes can have huge impacts on your life. Think of the "butterfly effect" theory, in which the tiniest flap of a butterfly's wings can cause a hurricane on the other side of the world.

That may not be strictly true, but we can all agree that making a small change can bring about a disproportionately impactful outcome.

Harness this truth and use it to your advantage: Make one small change to your surroundings and reap the benefits of your small effort!

If you're not sure what kind of change would work for this exercise, don't worry—your imagination is the only limit! However, if you're feeling stuck, here are a few ideas to get you started:

* Hang a new print on your wall, preferably one that you like to look at.
* Switch up the pictures you have displayed in the room. You can switch them out for new ones or simply move them around to create a fresh look.
* Rearrange the items on your desk to give the office a new feel.

Once you make your change, stand back and admire your handiwork. You'll find that making even the smallest of changes to your home or office can spark a new appreciation for the entire space.

CLEAN AND
ORGANIZE A ROOM

Cleaning may not be your favorite chore, but it's one that has the power to make you feel more productive, more positive, and more in control. Organizing has a similar impact and can make you feel even more efficient and more appreciative of your space.

If you're having trouble appreciating the room you're in, ask yourself this: Is it clean and tidy? Or is it messy, dirty, or unorganized? If the answer is "messy, dirty, or unorganized," you have a good indication of what exercise you should try next!

Once you have acknowledged that the room could use some sprucing up, make a plan of attack. Decide on what you will clean, tidy, and organize before you make your move. When you have a plan, get to it.

There is, however, one important thing to note—make sure you are hanging on to gratitude as you go about your chore. It can be easy to sink into grumbling about our tasks, especially with housework, but make an effort to stay grateful as you do it. Think about how you use the space and how well it serves you.

Once the room is spick-and-span, sit back and take a few minutes to simply enjoy your handiwork. Look around the room and cultivate a sense of gratitude for the space as well as the room's new tidiness!

FIRST–THING
MORNING GRATITUDE

You might think this exercise sounds like it's more suited for a morning person (and morning people will likely enjoy it), but actually this exercise is more for those people who would not classify themselves as morning people. In fact, it's *because* someone is not a morning person that this exercise can be so impactful for them!

Use this exercise to enhance your positivity and appreciation first thing in the morning—even when it's the last thing you feel like doing. Try this:

1. As soon as you wake up, turn off the alarm (or hit snooze, if you can't trust yourself to stay awake).
2. Instead of hopping up and getting ready for your day or checking your phone, take three minutes—just three minutes!—to simply lie in bed. Yes, this exercise is giving you permission to just lie in bed for a few minutes in the morning.
3. As you lie in your cozy bed, enjoying the warmth of just-slept-in bedding and allowing your eyes to adjust to the light, turn your mind to gratitude.
4. Cultivate a sense of gratitude for what's around you: the home that keeps you from being out on the streets, the bedroom that gives you a sense of privacy, the alarm clock that wakes you up for work in the morning, and so on.
5. If you have a tough time being grateful for these things, try being grateful for two of the most important things around you: your bed and your pillow! Say "thank you" for your comfy bed and your just-right pillow.

FIND INSPIRATION FROM YOUR IMMEDIATE ENVIRONMENT

Inspiration can be found all around you, if only you are willing to look! In order to cultivate a greater sense of gratitude for your surroundings, look at them with an eye toward inspiration.

If you're not sure how to get started, here's a handy guide:

1. Stop whatever you're doing. Hit the "pause" button on your brain, close your eyes, and take a moment to reframe your mind toward inspiration. Think about innovation, new ideas, and fresh perspectives.
2. Now open your eyes. Look around you, but don't look with your usual perspective—look with your new inspiration-colored glasses! Try to find something new, something fresh, something unusual.
3. Focus on at least one person or thing around you that gives you the most inspiration. Allow this person or thing to energize you, excite you, and encourage your imagination.
4. Come up with one idea, whether it's a practical, concrete idea or a lofty, abstract idea, based on the object of your attention. Follow this idea wherever it leads you.
5. Share your idea with someone. It doesn't need to be a grand, formal idea or a well-rehearsed spiel; just talk casually with someone about it.

You might think inspiration is supposed to strike at random, but it's actually far more likely to strike when you prepare and put in the effort. When you find inspiration in your surroundings, it's hard *not* to be grateful for them!

OFFER TO HELP SOMEONE ELSE

Do you know someone in your life who is struggling right now? Perhaps they're going through a messy divorce, dealing with unexpected job loss, or fighting a serious health issue. Whatever it is, chances are you know someone who could use your help.

Not only is it kind and compassionate to help someone in need; it also directly benefits the helper. When you offer your assistance to someone and they accept, it makes you feel useful, helpful, and appreciated. In turn, that increases your gratitude for that person.

So, think of someone in need and offer them help. Use these guidelines:

* Do your best not to make them feel ashamed or embarrassed about their circumstances. We all struggle sometimes, and it's inevitable that we will all need help once in a while.
* When you offer your assistance, be sincere and authentic. Don't say something like, "I guess I could help if you need it"; instead, say something like, "I'm happy to help you with anything you need."
* Be prepared to follow through; don't offer to help if you're not willing and able to actually help them.
* Be gracious, whether they accept or reject your offer. They may need help in ways that you can't provide, and that's okay.

PUT ON A
FRESH PERSPECTIVE

Sometimes feeling grateful for what is around you is as easy as putting on a fresh set of glasses. Not literal glasses, of course, but metaphorical glasses—although perhaps there's something to the idea of rose-colored glasses after all.

It can be really difficult to see the good things around you if you're totally used to seeing them every day. Donning a new pair of glasses, or putting on a fresh perspective, is one way to help you see the beauty of your surroundings and prompt greater gratitude.

Here's how to do it:

1. Think of someone who would find your current environment totally new—even foreign. This might be someone from another country, someone who grew up in a totally different environment (e.g., urban versus rural), or anyone with a vastly different perspective.
2. Imagine that this person's perspective is boiled down and manufactured into a pair of glasses. Get yourself a pair of these glasses and put them on!
3. Look around you with these glasses on, and see your surroundings with a fresh perspective. See the things you don't usually notice, like the print hanging on the wall of a coffee shop or the plants that are outgrowing their pots and spreading their lush green foliage.
4. Practice gratitude for each and every interesting, beautiful, and good thing you notice with your fresh perspective.

SLOW AND STEADY GRATITUDE STROLL

If you take frequent walks, you know that you can get some good thinking done on a walk. You probably also know how easy it is to slip into a state of mind where you're gazing off into the distance ahead of you but not really seeing it. That can be a sort of therapy on its own, but it's not conducive to cultivating greater gratitude for what's around you.

To go on a walk that *will* help you practice gratitude, try the following:

1. Set out with an intention to look around you and notice all there is to be grateful for.
2. Walk slowly and intentionally. You're not just trying to get from A to B; you're trying to enjoy yourself while you get there.
3. Be observant and pay attention to all the detail around you. It's natural to miss it when you're focused on something else, but on this walk you should make noticing it all your main priority. See the plants, the trees, the people, the animals, the street signs, the reflective paint on the road, and anything else that stands out as a noticeable detail.
4. Give thanks for all of these wonderful things that you notice, and be grateful for your ability to stop and "smell the roses" when you set your mind to it.

GO OUTSIDE—AND LEAVE
YOUR PHONE INSIDE

An easy way to be more observant and grateful of your surroundings is also one of the most difficult things for us to do: Leave our precious phones inside!

We've become addicted to our mobile devices, and there's good reason for it: They help us stay connected to each other, get our work done, learn new things, and stay entertained on the go.

However, they've made it all too easy to become a virtual zombie, walking around with no awareness of some of the best things around you.

To give yourself a break from your techno-zombie life, consider going outside and leaving your phone at home the next time you have a little free time. You could take a walk, go for a run, go on a hike, play with your children, take pictures (with an actual camera rather than your phone, of course), fly a kite, have a picnic—the options are nearly endless. What you do is not as important as the fact that you're doing something and being totally mindful while you do it.

Take advantage of the phone-free time to really pay attention to what's around you, and be thankful for your opportunity to enjoy it.

GET
OUT OF TOWN

One of the best ways to boost your gratitude for your surroundings is to put yourself in some pretty great surroundings.

Of course, there are a lot of ways to be more grateful for the "same old, same old" surroundings, but a quick trip to somewhere fun or exotic—or just to somewhere new—can give a quick boost to your gratitude. To take advantage of the benefits of going somewhere new, give this exercise a try.

Think about nearby locations that you've never been to before or places that are relatively close and really beautiful to visit. That might be a waterfall, a lake, a mountain, a city park, an amusement park, or even a neighboring city you've never been to. Although nature spots are popular for exercises like these, it's not necessary to go somewhere green to get the benefits of a new environment. A city block that you are unfamiliar with can even do in a pinch!

If you have the time now, go ahead and set off on your adventure! If not, plan out your excursion to this new locale. Whichever option you choose, make sure to keep your focus on noticing and appreciating the surroundings as you explore this new spot.

GO
BAREFOOT

Going barefoot is a great way to be more observant and aware of your surroundings—especially anything on the floor that you might step on—but it's also a good way to be more grateful for what is around you.

Although your feet are generally not as sensitive as your hands, you still carry a lot of nerve endings in them. That means that you can discern different textures and even explore and enjoy fun and interesting sensations with your feet.

Think about how it feels when you walk on the beach and the wet sand sucks up between your toes, or how the warm, dry sand provides an exfoliating sensation as you walk across it. If you have a beach nearby, take the time to head over and unlace your shoes for a bit!

Taking your shoes off and exploring the world around you is a fun outdoor activity that can help you appreciate fun textures, but don't underestimate the power of indoor barefoot experiences either.

Walking on a freshly polished hardwood floor can feel great on your feet, as can strolling through a room with lush, luxuriously soft carpet.

We often forget to use our feet when exploring and appreciating the world around us. Use this exercise to aid you in remembering, and be grateful for the ability to feel such marvelous sensations with your feet.

OPEN
YOUR EARS

Fortunately you can use all five senses to develop and maintain a healthy sense of gratitude. If you can hear, you can practice this simple exercise. If you are deaf or hard of hearing, skip over this exercise and flip to the pages ahead to see how you can use your other senses to build gratitude!

Follow these steps to use your ears to build greater gratitude for your surroundings:

1. Wherever you are, whatever you are doing right now, stop! Press pause and take a moment to yourself.
2. Close your eyes and inhale deeply through your nose, then exhale through your nose. Take three breaths like this and allow yourself to melt into the moment, staying mindful of what you are experiencing right here, right now.
3. Keeping your eyes closed, expand your awareness to your ears. Open them up to hearing everything around you—and actually *noticing* everything you hear!
4. Pay special attention to any sounds that are pleasant to hear. Try to isolate these sounds from the rest and appreciate them.
5. Build a feeling of gratitude for all the things you are able to experience through your ears.

When we're used to experiencing the world with all our senses, we get acclimated to all the good things we see, hear, smell, taste, and feel. Use exercises like this one to stay grateful for the amazing gift of each of your senses.

USE
YOUR NOSE

Continuing with the theme of using your senses to build your gratitude (see the previous exercise, "Open Your Ears"), this exercise focuses on another important sense: the sense of smell.

Our sense of smell is often underestimated, relegated to the role of enjoying a scented candle or the smell of dinner cooking but not much else; however, our sense of smell is an extremely powerful one.

Have you ever smelled something and immediately been transported back to another time in your life when you smelled that same scent? Chances are, you have. Your sense of smell is the sense that is most closely connected with your memory, so it's no surprise that this happens to you frequently.

Use this fact to your advantage and put your sense of smell to work building gratitude. Close your eyes and pay attention to what you can smell, focusing on anything that smells good or familiar.

If you recognize any of the smells, let yourself be taken back to any significant moments the smell brings up. Sink into the memories, savoring any that are positive or enjoyable to think about.

Cultivate a sense of gratitude for everything you can smell, and extend that gratitude to all of your surroundings.

FEEL
YOUR SURROUNDINGS

Just as in the previous two exercises ("Open Your Ears" and "Use Your Nose"), you can learn to use yet another sense to prompt gratitude in this exercise: your sense of touch.

We often forget to use this sense to appreciate and understand our world. Unlike puppies and babies, who absolutely *must* put anything interesting in their mouths to experience it, adult humans tend to pay attention to our senses of sight and hearing over the others when interacting with our environment.

However, ignoring your sense of touch can deprive you of a serious source of gratitude. To rectify this, use your sense of touch to experience your surroundings:

* Find something that looks nice to touch, and touch it! It might be something like a fuzzy blanket, your child's stuffed animal, or a silky curtain.
* Brush your fingers across things you don't usually touch, like the wall as you go upstairs or your smooth wood dining table as you walk by it.
* Grab something from your purse, backpack, or a junk drawer (as long as it doesn't have scissors!) without using your eyes. Reach your hand in and explore, challenging yourself to identify the object(s) you grab.

Give thanks for your sense of touch, and be grateful for the surroundings that give you an opportunity to put it to use.

SAVOR
SOMETHING DELICIOUS

Your sense of taste is perhaps the one that brings you the most joy in your everyday life, and it's one that can be easily employed to get an instant boost of happiness or gratitude.

If you've never heard of the activity called "savoring" before, here's a quick introduction: to savor something is to be completely aware of what you are doing and to keep your mind focused on the sensations you are experiencing, with a tendency toward the positive.

Here's how to savor something delicious:

1. Decide on something yummy to try for this exercise. Don't go with something you eat all the time or something you don't really enjoy; instead, pick something special, decadent, or truly delicious.
2. Set aside a few minutes to simply eat the food you've chosen, with no interruptions from kids, coworkers, or cell phones.
3. Take slow and mindful bites, chew several times, and swallow mindfully. Take your time to really experience and enjoy your food.
4. Pay attention to each distinct flavor, each different texture or mouthfeel, and the way it feels against your teeth.

Once you have finished your food, thank yourself for taking the time to savor something delicious!

THINK OF THE WORLD
AS A MOVIE SET

This is a fun and unique exercise that gives you a chance to recapture some of that childlike wonder about the world. Awe is an emotion we don't experience much as adults, but that doesn't mean it's completely inaccessible to us after a certain age.

Here's how you can regain your sense of wonder and cultivate gratitude for your surroundings:

1. Imagine that you are on a movie set or the set of a realistic television show. Imagine that each of the props, buildings, and costumes have been carefully and lovingly constructed.
2. Appreciate the detail that went into everything, from the rough feel of the building's bricks against your hand to the shine on the cars and the vivid colors of the clothing.
3. Allow yourself to notice things you don't usually notice, interact with things you usually ignore, and find joy in what you usually find mundane. Let yourself feel awe and wonder if that's what crops up!
4. Think about how much work went into building this set, and tell yourself to be grateful for the opportunity to explore it!

This exercise works by shifting your perspective on the world around you and prompting a more open-minded viewpoint. You'll be surprised by how much more you value what is around you when you simply make an effort to notice it!

LOOK OUT
THE WINDOW

This is a simple exercise, but it's also one of the most profound ones. We often think the more complicated or complex a thing is, the more impressive and effective it is; however, this viewpoint may cause us to forget to appreciate the simple and straightforward things in life.

To bring yourself back to the simple pleasures and things to be grateful for, try looking out the window:

1. Find a window near you, preferably with a view on nature, though that's not a "must-have."
2. Give yourself a few minutes to simply stare out the window. Let your eyes wander and land on whatever piques their interest.
3. For each thing you see, say a quick prayer or statement of gratitude. For example, if your eyes alight on a leaf, a person walking a dog, and a bird, give thanks for each in turn: "I am thankful for that beautiful leaf and the tree it came from. I am thankful for other people and for pets to keep us company. I am thankful for the birds that sing outside my window."
4. Continue for at least a few minutes, cultivating gratitude for each thing you see.

This exercise will not only help you be more grateful for your surroundings; it will also help you cultivate a more positive outlook on life in general.

WALK THROUGH
YOUR HOME

A simple but very effective way to feel more grateful for everything around you is to take a slow stroll through your home, opening yourself up to gratitude for everything you have.

Here's what to do:

1. Pick a time when you're alone in your home, if that's possible. It's easier to do this exercise when you aren't distracted.
2. Start in a room with two entrances, so you can start and stop in the same place.
3. Stand still for a moment, close your eyes, and set an intention to promote more gratitude for everything around you.
4. Now open your eyes and look around you, slowly scanning the room. Start walking slowly toward the next room, noting each of the things that catches your eye: a framed photograph of your family, the fridge, a coatrack.
5. Continue through each room until you have circled back to the start, noting everything you see. If it helps, you can use your sense of touch to physically mark each thing you're thinking of and feeling grateful for.
6. Once you reach your start/end point, make a quick mental inventory of all the things you noticed and cultivated gratitude for. Think of the many, many things on your list and let it all coalesce into one big feeling of gratitude for everything around you.

PLAY THE PART
OF PHOTOGRAPHER

You don't have to be a professional photographer to engage in this exercise; in fact, it's probably more fun and effective if you're a novice!

The point is not to actually take pictures but to develop a new viewpoint on your surroundings and a new appreciation for them.

Follow these steps to play the part of photographer:

1. Grab a camera or put an imaginary one around your neck.
2. Go hunting for subjects, whether they're alive or inanimate, inside or outside, big or small. Of course, if you're really taking pictures, make sure to get permission from any people you photograph.
3. Once you find a good subject, put the lens up to your eye and look through it. Notice what jumps out to you that didn't jump out to you before.
4. Next, take the lens away and give it another look. See the interesting, cool, unique, or beautiful aspects that you didn't notice before.
5. Now get to work! Take in your subject from every angle and direction, considering which is most flattering. Decide on where you'd like to begin snapping photos, and take a few (if you have a working camera).

Playing the part of a photographer helps us see things in a new light and appreciate things simply for their aesthetic appeal. Practice this regularly, and you will find yourself with a permanent shift in perspective to the positive and beautiful.

GO OUT
WITH FRIENDS

This is an easy one, right? How hard is it to go out with your friends! Generally, we find it pretty easy to go out with friends, and we enjoy many benefits from doing so: having fun, building connections, and enhancing our social skills.

However, going out with friends can also help you cultivate greater gratitude for everything around you.

To maximize the benefits of your day or evening out with friends, try to follow these guidelines:

* Pick a place with an interesting or interactive environment, like a museum or an innovative bar or club.
* Do something fun and new, if your friends are up for it. You might try playing laser tag, doing a wine and paint night, or going on an art walk in your city's downtown.
* Pay attention to your surroundings on your outing, and point interesting things out to your friends too.
* Allow yourself to be excited and engaged with your friends and with everything around you, even if it doesn't seem "cool."

The mix of the familiar and fun (your friends) with the novel and exciting (your surroundings) will compel you to naturally feel more gratitude for what you see and interact with. Be sure to complement this natural boost with some mindful effort on feeling more grateful.

EXERCISES TO CULTIVATE GRATITUDE IN DIFFICULT TIMES

Although tough times are the most difficult contexts in which to practice and enhance your gratitude, they are the best times to do so. Think about it: If you can practice gratitude when you feel like your world is crashing down around you, will there ever come a time when you *can't* practice it? This chapter takes this concept and runs with it, offering you twenty-five ways to cultivate gratitude in difficult times. Exercises include reminding yourself of your past successes and accomplishments, reaching out to your support system, counting blessings instead of burdens, and finding ways to apply what you are learning to a more positive future.

CATALOG YOUR
LESSONS LEARNED

It might sound cliché, but it's true that you can find peace and gratitude in the lessons learned from your struggles. You may find it difficult to focus on the good during trying times, but you may have better luck staying grateful if you view things from this perspective.

In the midst of your troubles, grab your notebook or pen and paper and write yourself a list of all the things you've learned—things you've learned about yourself, about life, about others, and so on.

For example, if you're going through a divorce, you might write:

* I have learned that I can't be with someone who has X trait or Y habit.
* I have learned that I am much stronger and more capable than I thought.
* I have learned that time really does take the sting out of your pain—slowly but surely.

Once you have a list of at least five or six lessons learned, read through your list again and cultivate gratitude for each lesson learned. Repeat this aloud or in your head for each lesson: "I am grateful that I have learned…"

Finish up your list and say this to yourself: "I'm struggling now, but I am grateful for what I have learned and I will be better equipped to handle struggles the next time they pop up."

REMIND YOURSELF OF PAST SUCCESS

One of the key methods to getting through a difficult time with grace and gratitude is to keep your focus on the positive. For this exercise, you can keep your positive focus by thinking about your past successes.

Think about what you are going through right now. Consider how and why it's as difficult as it is—does it challenge you emotionally, mentally, physically, or perhaps in all three ways?

When you have a handle on why this time is so difficult for you, think back to another time when you struggled. This past event should be something that challenged you in similar ways. For example, if you're struggling with the death of a loved one, think back to how you handled a previous loss.

Remind yourself of how you got through that event. Remember how difficult it felt at the time? Maybe you felt like you wouldn't be able to get through it—but remind yourself that you did. You survived and have no doubt thrived at some point since then. Give yourself some gratitude for making it through last time, and cultivate gratitude for the ability to get through it again now.

If it helps, give yourself a little pep talk based on your past success. You might say something like, "I know this feels impossible now, but remember when it felt impossible before? And you got through it! You can do it again."

REACH OUT TO SOMEONE WHO UNDERSTANDS

A support system is one of the most important resources you can have when you're trying to get through a tough time. Having someone to talk to, cry to, and lean on can make all the difference. While anyone who will listen and commiserate is a great resource right now, there are some people who will be especially helpful: people who truly understand.

These people have likely gone through something similar in their own lives, giving them the wisdom and perspective on your situation that you simply haven't had time to develop yet.

Reach out to someone like this. Text, call, video chat with, or visit her or him in person if you can. Ask for any advice, support, or encouragement this person can provide.

As you listen to him or her and try to glean some valuable tips, focus on how grateful you are to have this person in your life. Feel every bit of gratitude that comes up as you enjoy this person's company, and share your gratitude with him or her.

To boost your gratitude experience, take a few minutes after meeting with your friend or mentor and write down how great it was to have his or her help in getting through whatever stress you're dealing with. Write a letter telling this person exactly how she or he helped and just how grateful you are, and drop the letter in the mail or deliver it by hand.

COUNT THE THINGS
YOU STILL HAVE

Have you ever heard the phrase "Count your blessings, not your burdens"? It can be tough advice to follow in the best of times, but when we're struggling with something particularly difficult, it can feel downright impossible.

To make it a little easier to cultivate gratitude for your blessings, follow these steps:

1. Think about what you're struggling with right now; is it your relationship with your spouse or significant other? Perhaps it's a stressful situation at work or a health issue. Determine what area(s) of life it is affecting.

2. Now that you have an idea of which area(s) you are struggling in, think about all the *other* areas of your life where you are not. If your issue is your relationship with your spouse, think about your more stable and happy relationships with your kids, your parents, other family members, or friends. If you're struggling with work, think about your good health and happy home life.

3. Count all the things you still have—in other words, the things that are still going right. Cultivate gratitude for all those things that *could* be going wrong but aren't. Say a prayer, meditate, or simply share your gratitude for these good things in your life with the universe.

MAKE A LIST OF YOUR SOURCES OF SUPPORT

When you are feeling down, it can be tough to remember all the people who are there for you. They say that "no man is an island," and generally this is true; it's exceedingly rare to find someone who has no sources of love and support. As lonely as you may feel sometimes, there is someone out there whom you can lean on in a crisis, and this exercise will help you remember that.

Take a few minutes, sit down with a notebook and a pen, and follow these steps:

1. First, think about your closest and dearest sources of support: your spouse or significant other, your parents, your children, your siblings, grandparents, and so on. This is your "first line" of support.
2. Next, list your other close sources of support: dear friends, cousins, aunts and uncles, other non-immediate relatives, mentors and/or mentees, and colleagues you who are especially close with.
3. Finally, think about the fringe sources of support. These are the people you may not turn to immediately in a crisis, but you can lean on them or share your burden with them if you need to. These sources of support can vary widely from person to person: your boss, your hairdresser, an old teacher or coach, a neighbor, or a pastor/priest/rabbi.
4. Count up all of these sources of support, and let yourself feel lucky and loved. Keep the list to refer back to in your toughest moments.

THINK AHEAD TO THE
NEXT EPISODE

Life can be cyclical—sometimes the thing you struggle with in one period of life can come back in a new or updated form. For example, the heartbreak of your first relationship ending is mirrored in a marriage or other long-term relationship ending as an adult. The situations are different, but some of the underlying feelings are the same.

When you're in the middle of something particularly tough, try to think about what you will learn from this experience that you can apply to the next "episode" or the next time a similar problem comes up. Think about the skills you have gained or sharpened, the things you've learned about yourself and the world around you, and the techniques you have added to your toolbox.

Consider how the next episode will go more smoothly because of what you have learned. Look ahead and feel gratitude for what you are gaining right now and how it will ease your burden in the future.

It's unfortunate that you may have to experience some of the more negative parts of life many times over, but there's also an upside—this means you have the advantage of learning from the first go-round and applying what you have learned to the next episode.

FIND A
COMPARISON SCENARIO

This is not your typical "think of something positive" sort of exercise. We're going to go a little dark and absurd. Are you ready for it?

If you want to fast-track your gratitude, even in some of the most difficult times of your life, try coming up with a comparison scenario.

Think about what's going wrong in your life right now. Is it something at work? Maybe you have a really difficult boss or a challenging project that's sapping all your energy. Or is it something in your personal relationships? It might be a bad breakup or a rough patch with your spouse.

Whatever it is, get a good image of your current situation in your mind. Now compare your current scenario to one that's way worse.

If your current issue is a difficult boss, think of these alternate scenarios:

* Your whole team is now composed of several versions of your boss.
* Your boss follows you home and lives with you in your house every night.
* You don't have a job at all, but your boss goes everywhere you go, nitpicking everything you do.

These scenarios can be absurd, totally realistic, or somewhere in between; the only rule is that they must be worse than your current situation.

When you have a good one in mind, compare it to what you're dealing with right now, and you'll find that you're grateful to be grappling with your current problem!

FIND GRATITUDE FOR THE WELL-BEING OF OTHERS IN YOUR LIFE

When you simply can't find the strength or the willpower to practice gratitude for your own situation, it can feel hopeless to try to feel any gratitude at all. It can become very difficult to feel grateful for anything when you're down in the dumps, but it's not impossible to feel *any* gratitude.

If you're finding it extraordinarily hard to be grateful for your own situation, find solace in being grateful that others in your life are happy and well.

Follow these guidelines to try finding gratitude for others:

1. Think of two or three people you love dearly, people who are important in your life.
2. Take a few minutes to jot down some notes about what is going well for these people. For example, you might choose to think of your wife and her recent success in her career. Repeat for each person on your list.
3. Cultivate gratitude for the positive circumstances surrounding each of these people. Put your gratitude into words. For example, you might say out loud, "I am grateful that my wife is doing so well at work right now." Repeat for each person on your list.

Find something to be sincerely grateful for regarding each of your loved ones, and you'll see that it's easier to cultivate gratitude than you thought.

VISUALIZE
THE GOOD

Visualization is a powerful tool that can help you boost your mood, accomplish your goals, and plan for the future. It's also an effective tool for helping you foster gratitude and fight your way through, even in the most difficult of times.

When you're feeling low, putting your imagination to work visualizing the good things in life can be exactly what you need to keep going.

Follow these steps to visualize the good:

1. Find a quiet, peaceful spot, like your bedroom or an empty office.
2. Get comfortable—but not so comfortable that you'll fall asleep—and close your eyes.
3. Think about some of the best things you have experienced in life. If you have trouble bringing them to mind, think of your favorite things, places, and people. Do you have some great memories or maybe a "happy place" to dwell on?
4. Choose one good thing to visualize and activate your imagination. Think of your one good thing in as much detail as possible and re-create it in your mind's eye. For example, if your good thing is your living room on Christmas Eve, imagine the entire scene: the tree glistening with lights and ornaments, the fire crackling, the smell of hot buttered rum, and the sound of your children's laughter. Make it as real as possible, and stay with your one good thing for a while.

Let that goodness seep into you, and carry it with you when you open your eyes and continue on with your day.

GO HUNTING
FOR THE POSITIVE

Did you like to go on scavenger hunts when you were a kid? There's nothing like the thrill of solving a clever clue or picking up on a small detail that leads you to your prize.

You can use this exercise to engage that sense of fun, challenge, and excitement while enhancing your gratitude at the same time.

To give it a shot, all you need to do is be willing to put in a little effort and engage your imagination. You're about to go on a scavenger hunt for positive things in your life, and the grand prize is to be a happier and more positive version of yourself.

To get started, get a pen and some paper and write down the rules. You can use the rules that follow or make them up to suit your preferences.

1. You must stop what you are doing and find at least three positive things, three times a day.
2. You must find these nine positive things per day for one week.
3. You can't duplicate any positive things (e.g., all sixty-three things need to be unique).

The positive things don't need to be big things; you might find positive things like, "A stranger held the door for me and smiled at me" or "I found a quarter on the ground."

Each day, be on the lookout for positive things, and you'll win the prize of gratitude!

ENVISION A BIG BALL OF GRATITUDE

When you feel overwhelmed and buried in stress and negativity, you need something big to get your head into the right place for gratitude. This exercise is exactly that!

Do you ever use visualization? If not, you might want to flip back a few pages and try the exercise "Visualize the Good." If you already use visualization, you'll be well-prepared for this exercise.

To create and use your big ball of gratitude, here's what you do:

1. Find a quiet place, close your eyes, and relax.
2. Think of the very best, most beloved, most cherished things in your life, like your relationship with your children and/or your spouse. Channel that pure goodness into a little ball of beautiful, glowing light in your hand.
3. Hold the ball and think of a few other good things, like your joy when you engage in a favorite hobby. Send that into the ball too.
4. Continue adding goodness to the ball and watch as it grows bigger and bigger. See all that you have to be grateful for in this pulsing ball of light.
5. Allow it to become so big, it swallows you up. Stand inside this big ball of gratitude and allow it to soak all the way into you. Imagine absorbing all of the gratitude in this ball.
6. Open your eyes, feel the gratitude inside, and carry it with you as you go about your business.

START WITH JUST ONE GOOD THING

If you're having trouble thinking of anything good, don't be discouraged. It's natural to feel frustrated and downtrodden when you're going through tough times, and that can make it extremely difficult to bring anything positive to mind.

If that describes the way you're feeling, try this: Start with just *one* thing.

Really, that's it! Just one thing. It can be extremely small. It can be seemingly insignificant. It can even be something good that happened to someone else. All you need to do is come up with one teeny, tiny positive thing and focus on it for a moment or two.

You might be thinking this exercise sounds deceptively easy. Shouldn't there be more to it?

No, and here's why: Sometimes all you need to pull through is the reminder that there *is* good out there, somewhere in the world. It doesn't need to be anything monumental, and it doesn't need to be personal. You just need one small speck of proof that good actually exists to open you up to the possibility of good things in your own life.

So, if you're feeling truly down, pull together just enough willpower and effort to think of just one good thing, and give yourself a pat on the back when you do. The gratitude will follow in time.

HELP
SOMEONE ELSE

Why do people volunteer?

There are a lot of answers to that question, but I think the biggest one is the simplest one: It feels good to help other people.

We're truly lucky there's such a surefire way to make ourselves feel better! And even luckier that there are so many ways to go about it.

Here are just a few examples of ways you can help someone else:

* Volunteer at a soup kitchen.
* Donate your gently used clothing to a family in need.
* Give money to a worthy local cause.
* Help a friend move during a tough time in his or her life.
* Visit an elderly family member or neighbor and offer to do some chores for this person.

It's great to help others, no matter what the reason; however, to make sure you are getting your boost of gratitude from this experience, make sure to follow it up with some reflection:

1. Think about how it felt to do what you did. Name the emotions you felt (e.g., proud, warm and fuzzy, joyful).
2. Think about the concrete ways your actions helped the other person(s).
3. Be grateful that you have the ability to engage in this positive action and do something good for another person.

Helping someone else makes you feel good and puts you on the other side of gratitude, which paradoxically makes it easier for you to be grateful yourself.

ENGAGE IN AN ACTIVITY YOU EXCEL AT

What's your special talent or skill? Can you recite all fifty US states at lightning speed? Are you an accomplished guitar player? Do you kill at trivia night?

Whatever activity you're good at—no matter how seemingly insignificant—you probably really enjoy doing it, right? Of course you do! It's always fun to be good at something.

During tough times, it can be easy to lose sight of the things you are good at and the things you enjoy doing. To keep your spirits up and stay grateful, commit to engaging in an activity you excel at. For example:

* If you are great at soccer, sign up for a local recreational team or offer to be an assistant coach for your kid's team.
* If you're an excellent cook, plan and execute an extravagant six-course meal. It could be for a dinner party, just for you and your significant other, or just for yourself.
* If you regularly score more than two hundred points when bowling, join a league or set up a weekly bowling night with friends.

By engaging in something you're good at, you remind yourself that you really do have skills and talents to be grateful for. Plus, you'll have some fun doing it—it's a win-win!

REMIND YOURSELF OF THE TRUTH ABOUT GRATITUDE

This may be one of the most important exercises in the entire book, because it hinges on one fundamental, essential, vital truth about gratitude.

What truth is that?

It's this: Being grateful for your current situation is the key to happiness, not getting exactly what you want out of life.

I know, that probably sounds familiar. You might be thinking that this isn't such a big secret, that it's an obvious truth. But is it?

How often do you see people complaining about their circumstances, bemoaning fate or destiny or other people for keeping them from getting the thing they want? How often do you see already-wealthy people grasping for more and more? How often do you see people refusing the more well-paying job because they like their simple job and simple life?

It's not bad to aim high and work hard to get what you want, but the most important truth about gratitude is that being content and grateful for everything you have, right here and right now, is the only way to be truly happy.

If you're thinking, "Sure, I'll be grateful and happy as soon as X or Y happens," remind yourself that this simply isn't true. Learn to be happy with what you have, and you will protect yourself against the ups and downs of changing circumstances.

COMMIT
TO FLEXIBILITY

Are you ready to hear the secret to building and maintaining gratitude as a trait? It's flexibility!

The secret to becoming a more grateful, happier, and healthier person is to commit to being flexible. It can be hard to be flexible when we're struggling, but this is when it's most important—and most impactful—to being flexible in our gratitude practice.

Being flexible when it comes to practicing gratitude means several things:

* Give yourself a break when you miss a scheduled gratitude session or forget to practice at some point. It happens to all of us at some point!
* Be willing to change up your planned gratitude practice at the last minute; you might plan to show gratitude for your past, but if something comes up that contributes to gratitude for others, feel free to update your practice.
* Allow yourself to be interrupted during your practice. It will happen at some point, and it's no reason to get upset—it's a perfect opportunity to apply what you have learned about gratitude in a real-world context.
* Keep your practice fluid and be willing to make the changes necessary to better suit your needs. You might need to work on self-gratitude now, but don't limit yourself to that if you need to work on staying grateful in tough times in the future!

Commit yourself to being flexible; that's the secret to building and maintaining a trait of gratitude, even through tough times.

GET IN
SOME CUDDLE TIME

Are you a cuddler—one of those people who could just cuddle up next to someone you love all day long? If so, you'll like this exercise! If not, you should give it a shot, for the sake of enhanced gratitude if for nothing else.

This exercise is good for building gratitude any time, but it can be extra effective when you're dealing with something difficult in your life. Cuddling with someone you love can release the feel-good chemicals in your brain that remind you there are indeed things to be grateful for in your life.

To get in your dose of cuddle time, find a partner and engage in one of these tried-and-true cuddling positions:

* **Big spoon, little spoon:** One person wraps their arms around the other from behind; can be done lying down or standing up.
* **The honeymoon hug:** Each person faces the other and wraps their arms around the other person (and legs too, if it's with your romantic partner).
* **The lap pillow:** Lay your head in the other person's lap; this is a great position for feeling comforted.
* **The sitting arm wrap:** Sit side by side and put your closest arm around the other person's back; this is a good position for those who are not romantically involved but still want to get the benefits of cuddling!

MAKE YOURSELF YOUR FAVORITE MEAL

Sometimes just doing a little something nice for yourself can give you a boost of gratitude, even when you feel like you have nothing to be grateful for. Try making yourself a truly excellent meal to give yourself something to be thankful about!

The exercise is as simple as it sounds—just making yourself a meal—but there are a few caveats:

* It has to be a homemade meal, not store-bought. Ordering takeout or getting pizza delivered definitely doesn't count!
* It has to be one of your absolute favorite meals; no skimping or substituting a boring salad or sandwich!
* It has to be something that takes more than a few minutes to throw together; if it stretches your cooking skills too, all the better!

Make sure you give yourself time to sit down and think about what you want to make, plan out your recipes, and pick up all the ingredients you need at the grocery store. If you find yourself rushing out to the store in the middle of cooking to pick up that one ingredient you don't have, you're far less likely to enjoy the experience and feel more grateful!

If you plan it out and treat yourself like an honored guest in your own home, you'll make yourself feel special, appreciated, and even a bit pampered. Take those feelings and use them to remind yourself that there is always something that can brighten your day, even in the darkest of times.

THINK OF
THE RAINBOW

"You can't have a rainbow without some rain." Yes, this is a cliché, but it has a valuable kernel of truth in it.

We all know this is true, but we don't always *feel* that it's true. It's nothing to be ashamed of or upset about; we're human, and we sometimes have trouble seeing past our discouraging immediate circumstances to the good things right around the corner.

This exercise can help you get that perspective you need to pull yourself out of a funk and maintain a sense of gratitude, even when it's the last thing you feel capable of doing.

Here's what you do:

1. When you're having a particularly low moment, remind yourself of the saying "You can't have a rainbow without some rain."
2. Think about how it applies in your life. It might not seem readily apparent, but just give it some thought, and you'll see that there are some good things in your life that came from the bad. For example, maybe you failed out of college, but you met your spouse at the job you took after that. Or perhaps you were fired from a job only to end up at one you liked much more.
3. Identify your rainbows, and remind yourself that this is the rain—but that means a rainbow is on the horizon!

PUSH OUT
THE BITTERNESS

Bitterness is a sneaky pattern of thinking and feeling that likes to slowly insinuate itself into your life. You might let in just a *little* bit of bitterness when you're having a bad day, only to find out later that it has seeped into every corner of your mind and now rears its ugly head all the time!

To make room for meaningful, to-the-core gratitude in your life, you first need to address all the bitterness and empty it out.

Here's a visualization technique to help you do it:

1. Find a quiet spot to sit and think, and seek out your bitterness. Where is it hiding? Where did it come from? What is it concerned about?

2. Visualize your bitterness in your mind. The exact imagery you see will vary, but you might envision something like a cup filled with battery acid, a big ball of sludge, or a pool of poison sloshing around in your mind.

3. Make the conscious decision to empty out all the bitterness, and imagine it happening. See yourself emptying the cup down the drain, pushing the ball out of your mind, or using a hose to suction out the pool of it.

4. As you watch the bitterness recede or disappear, release all the bitterness inside you. Watch a cleansing wave of forgiveness sweep the last remnants out of your mind and clean it of any residue.

ACCEPT
THE EFFORT REQUIRED

Acceptance is one of the keys to happiness. It's virtually impossible to be truly content if you cannot accept yourself as you are, accept others as they are, and accept your reality.

People often get "accepting" confused with "condoning," but they are not the same. You do not have to like, approve of, or feel good about reality to accept it; you just need to acknowledge that "it is what it is."

Acceptance also plays a role in your gratitude practice. You might think that practicing gratitude should be easy and carefree, simply a way of life that you choose once and never look back from; however, that is unfortunately not how it works. Being truly grateful takes time, effort, and energy—but it's worth it.

For this exercise, work on:

* Accepting that being grateful requires effort.
* Carving out the time and space to practice gratitude.
* Believing that tough times are the best times to practice gratitude!

Cultivating a practice of gratitude in your life—no matter what the circumstances—requires effort, and there's no time like the difficult or draining present to get started. If you can form a healthy new habit in some of your darkest days, there's good reason to believe that you will be able to make it stick!

SET SOME
GRATITUDE GOALS

Setting goals is a necessary activity for anyone who wants to improve or enhance themselves—and don't we all want to improve ourselves? Without goal-setting, there is no way to measure your progress or determine if you've actually met your goal. Plus, it's a lot easier to stay motivated when you can see tangible proof of your progress, even if it's just some marks on a piece of paper or boxes checked.

If you want to enhance your sense of gratitude—especially during tough times when it's *really* difficult to do—take advantage of the benefits of goal-setting to help you get there.

Here's how to set some gratitude goals that will assist you in boosting your gratitude:

1. Think about how much gratitude you feel for yourself and your life right now. If it helps, you can rate it on a scale from one to ten.
2. Think about how far you have to go before you'll feel like you have a good amount of gratitude.
3. Decide on a certain amount of practice, number of activities, or schedule of exercises that you believe will help you get to your goal.
4. Make it official! Write down where you are now, where you'd like to be, and how you plan to get there. If you have a gratitude journal, that's a good place to write it all down.
5. Commit to practicing gratitude as described in your journal entry—and make sure to follow through.

ENVISION YOURSELF AS
A STUDENT OF LIFE

It might sound a little corny, but envisioning yourself as a "student of life" can help you deal with the stress of a tough situation. Sometimes the way your life goes after disappointment or disaster is about your perspective more than anything else.

If you want to try out a new perspective, this exercise is a great way to do it. Follow these steps to give it a shot:

1. Envision yourself as a student or a scholar, or perhaps even a researcher or investigator. If it helps, see yourself in the clothing you think would be appropriate, in a setting that vibes (like a library or a cozy office with books on the shelf).
2. Now that you have a clear image in your head, imagine yourself doing the work: taking notes, reading up on the subject, or having in-depth discussions with colleagues about it.
3. Remind yourself that the subject is life! As you endure difficult moments, upsetting experiences, and downright traumatic events, remember that you can always pull back and take a different perspective: that of the objective and curious observer.
4. Think about what lessons you can learn from each obstacle that comes your way, and cultivate a sense of gratitude for each and every one of them. Write them down if that helps.

Of course, it's not good to be totally detached and objective about what happens to you all the time, but it can be an excellent tool for coping with difficult situations while also building gratitude.

FACE YOUR
OWN MORTALITY

It seems counterintuitive, but thinking about the fragility of life can be an incredibly empowering and encouraging experience!

This exercise is a way to work on changing your perspective and inviting more gratitude into your life, and it can be done at any time.

Here's how to do it:

1. When you're dealing with your darkest days or most difficult moments, remind yourself of this fact: Your time on this earth is limited, and one day you will no longer be here to experience any of the highs or lows of life as a human being.
2. Think about all the highs you would have missed out on: the day you graduated or got your first really important job, the day you got married, the day your child was born, or any of the other "highs" in life.
3. Think about the lows you're experiencing now, and acknowledge that things could probably be worse. Remind yourself that you will probably be over this period in your life and better for it within a year or perhaps even less time.

It may sound morbid, but most people find that thinking about their own mortality has a strong, positive impact—it makes you appreciate what you have now, even if it doesn't seem that great.

In other words, it helps you tell yourself, "Sure, things seem bad now, but look at you—you're alive and kicking!"

GET SOME
PERSPECTIVE

The final exercise in this book will help you get some perspective. Many of the other exercises touch on this, but this one will dedicate its entire focus to broadening your horizons and gaining new perspective.

Here's what to do:

1. Think of another difficult time, one when you thought you might not be able to make it through. This should be a time that was at least a year or two ago, and ideally one that wasn't quite as dire as your mind wanted to make it.
2. Consider this difficult time and ask yourself these questions about it:
   * Do you ever think about this difficult time now?
   * How often do you think about it?
   * Does this difficult time still impact you on a daily basis?
   * Did anything positive come from this experience?
3. You will probably find that your answers to these questions paint a certain picture: one of your circumstances seeming totally unbearable and life-altering at the time, but seeming much tamer and less impactful after the fact. Remind yourself of this fact and try to apply it to your current experience.

When you back up a few steps and get some perspective, you often realize that things aren't as bad as they seem and that you are more capable of getting through it than you think. Cultivate a feeling of gratitude for the difficult experiences that prepared you for what you are facing today, and try to extend that gratitude to your current struggles as well.

INDEX